H

D0386861

WILLIAM PENN

Quaker Colonist

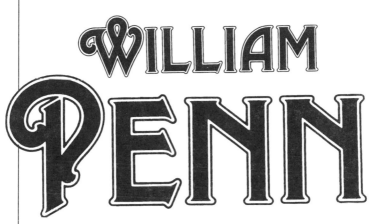

WILLIAM PENN

Quaker Colonist

KIERAN DOHERTY

The Millbrook Press
Brookfield, Connecticut

Photographs courtesy of The Granger Collection: pp. 16, 47, 107, 162-163 © National Maritime Museum Picture Library, Greenwich, London: p. 23; The Historical Society of Pennsylvania: pp. 50, 73, 113, 146; Culver Pictures: pp: 52-53, 67; The Pennsylvania Academy of the Fine Arts, Philadelphia. Gift of Mrs. Sarah Harrison (The Joseph Harrison, Jr. Collection): p. 115; Haverford College Library: Quaker Collection: p. 138

Library of Congress Cataloging-in-Publication Data
Doherty, Kieran.
William Penn : Quaker colonist / Kieran Doherty.
p.   cm.
Includes bibliographical references and index.
Summary: A biography of William Penn, founder of the Quaker colony of Pennsylvania, who struggled throughout his life for the freedom to practice his religion.
ISBN 0-7613-0355-3 (lib. bdg.)
1. Penn, William, 1644–1718—Juvenile literature. 2. Pioneers—Pennsylvania—Biography—Juvenile literature. 3. Quakers—Pennsylvania—Biography—Juvenile literature. 4. Pennsylvania—History—Colonial period, ca. 1600–1775—Juvenile literature. [1. Penn, William, 1644–1718. 2. Quakers. 3. Pennsylvania—History—Colonial period, ca. 1600–1775.]
I. Title.
F152.2.D73   1998
974.8'02'092—dc21
[B]   97-48504   CIP   AC

Published by The Millbrook Press, Inc.
2 Old New Milford Road
Brookfield, Connecticut

1   3   5   6   4   2

For my wife, Lynne,
and my sons, Dylan and Eamon

Contents

If we would amend the world, we should
mend Our selves; and teach our children to be,
not what we are, but what they should be.

William Penn,
"Some Fruits of Solitude"

ONE

A Sea Captain's Son

On October 12, 1644, an English man-of-war named the *Fellowship* eased away from the docks that lined the Thames River at the center of London. Under the command of twenty-three-year-old Captain William Penn, the ship was bound for Ireland where her twenty-eight big cannons would be used to wage war against rebellious Irish Catholics.

Pushed along by the ebbing tide, the ship wove her way down the river, scattering ducks and geese and swans as she passed. Accompanied by the shouts of rivermen who cried, "Oars! Oars! Oars!" as they advertised the services of the rowboats that carried passengers up and down the river, the ship soon left the city's center behind.

As the *Fellowship* made her way toward the river's mouth and the open ocean beyond, Captain Penn paced the quarterdeck at the vessel's stern. He turned often to look back in the direction of Tower Hill where he lived with his wife in a comfortable house within sight of the Tower of London. In that house, Margaret Penn was about to give birth to their first child.

About a dozen miles down the river the crew of the *Fellowship* let go the vessel's anchors, and she came to rest near the large dockyard at Deptford. There, on October 14, a messenger sent from London reached the ship with word that Margaret Penn's labor had started. The captain rushed back to the city. By the time he reached his wife's side, the baby, a healthy boy, had entered the world.

Following the baby's birth, the *Fellowship*'s sailing was delayed for about two weeks. On October 23, Captain Penn carried his son to All Hallows Church on Tower Street, around the corner from the Penn house. A simple note in the parish registry shows that the "sonn of william pen & margaret his wife" was baptized into the Anglican faith on that day. The boy was given the name William, like his father, grandfather, and great-grandfather before him.

The England into which young William Penn was born was a nation torn by civil war. On one side in the war were King Charles I and his supporters, called "Royalists." These were mostly aristocrats and members of the ruling class. Since most of these men wore their hair long and dressed in fancy clothes, they were known as "Cavaliers" by their opponents. On the other side were the "Parliamentarians." Many of these were commoners. Since these men cut their hair short, they were called "Roundheads" by the Cavaliers.

The English Civil War had two basic causes. First, it was a struggle to decide who would govern England. Edward Hyde, the earl of Clarendon, who lived through the war to become one of England's most famous historians, put it simply when he said the war was fought to determine "whether the King was above

Parliament, or Parliament, in ruling, [was] above the King."[1]

But the Civil War was also about religion, specifically about the way the Anglican Church, the official state church in England, was organized.

The Parliamentarians were, by and large, Puritans. They got this name because they wanted to purify the Anglican Church by cleansing it of all traces of Roman Catholicism. They also wanted more say in the way church affairs were handled. Most Royalists, on the other hand, wanted to keep the Anglican faith as it was, with its bishops and vestiges of Catholicism and with the ruler of England as its earthly leader.

In 1644, when the younger William Penn was born, the Civil War had been going on for two years. Under the leadership of Oliver Cromwell, the Parliamentarian army had just won a great victory at the battle of Marston Moor. Charles I and his court had been forced to flee from London to the walled city of Oxford. Henrietta Marie, the French princess who became the Queen of England when she married Charles I, had fled her adopted land and was in exile at the court of King Louis XIV in France.

The war forced English men and women to take sides. For Captain Penn this had not been an easy chore. Though he was a Royalist who wanted the monarchy preserved, he was, first, a navy officer. His duty, as far as he was concerned, was to protect England from attack by outsiders. He was, his son later said, led by "national concern and not domestic issues. . . ."[2]

Several days after young William's baptism, Captain Penn set sail for the Irish Sea. For the next five years, he was rarely at home. Most of the time, he was off fighting Irish Catholics who threatened to send troops to England to fight for the King. In those years, the captain proved himself an able and brave mariner. That was not surprising, since he had gone to sea as a boy aboard his father's merchant ship and had taken command of his own vessel when he was just seventeen. He was, his son later said, "addicted from his youth to maritime affairs."[3] His exploits attracted the attention of Cromwell himself, and soon Captain Penn was promoted, first to vice admiral and later to admiral of the Irish Sea.

With the captain gone, Margaret and young William lived in the house on Tower Hill. Located within the old city wall, the house consisted of "one hall and parlor and kitchen with a divided cellar . . . and above stairs in the first story two fair chambers and in the second story two more chambers and two garrets over the same with a yard before."[4]

Those were hard, uncertain times for Margaret Penn, alone in London with a newborn baby. The city, like most large cities in Europe in those days, was crowded and dirty and ridden with disease. Money was scarce, for Parliament often had no funds to pay soldiers' and sailors' wages. As a Parliamentarian stronghold, there was always a chance that London might be attacked by Royalist forces.

At about the age of three, William came down with smallpox. This disease, which has now been virtually wiped out around the world, regularly ravaged cities like London in the seventeenth century, killing many of its victims. Young William, however, survived, though the illness did cause him to lose most of his hair.

Even in the midst of war and want, the house on Tower Hill was not a gloomy place, for Margaret Penn was a strong woman who had experienced hard times before and not lost her sense of humor. The daughter of a London businessman named John Jasper, she had married a Dutch merchant when she was still a teenager. She and her first husband were living in the Dutch-English colony of Kilrush in Ireland when her husband died. She was still there when, in 1641, war broke out between Irish Catholics and Protestants. Threatened by that war, she fled for London, leaving behind a large estate she inherited from her husband. In London, she met Captain Penn and married him about fourteen months before young William was born.

By all accounts, Margaret was a fun-loving woman. She enjoyed practical jokes and laughter and song. Samuel Pepys, the famous English diarist who later lived near the Penn family, said that on one occasion Margaret "flung me down upon the bed, and herself and others, one after another, [tickled] me, and very merry we were. . . ."[5] She was also easygoing when it came to housekeeping and did not pay much attention to the cleanliness and order of her clothes. She walked around her house, Pepys reported, "with her stockings hanging round her heels."[6]

It is easy to imagine this easygoing, fun-loving woman spoiling young William a bit after his illness, perhaps singing to him or telling him stories of Ireland and the estate she'd lost. She probably smiled to herself as she thought that her husband, Captain Penn, was, even as she spoke, fighting some of the same rebellious Irish Catholics who had taken her estate.

During the first five years of young William's life, much changed in England. The Civil War came to an end. Oliver Cromwell became the nation's ruler. King Charles I was captured and beheaded by the Parlia-

The artist who drew this picture in the mid-1600s was obviously an ardent Royalist—though Charles II became King of Great Britain in 1648 when his father was executed, he did not actually rule his people until 1660.

mentarians. The King's sons, Charles II and James, the duke of York who was later to become King James II, lived in exile to avoid the executioner's axe or a dank and dirty cell in the Tower of London.

During this period, not long after young William's bout with smallpox, William's father came home on leave and moved his wife and son to a spacious house near the village of Wanstead, about ten miles from London. His visit was brief, for no sooner had the Royalist forces surrendered than war started between England and Holland. The senior Penn, now an admiral, was sent to fight in the Mediterranean.

In Wanstead, William found a life very different from the one he'd known in London. Instead of living in a narrow house with rooms stacked one on top of the other, they lived in a spacious manor. The fresh, country air smelled of grass and flowers and grain instead of "the fumes, steams and stinks"[7] that one Londoner said lay over much of London. Instead of crowded, narrow streets overhung with wooden buildings that leaned against each other drunkenly and gutters littered with trash, there were open fields where sheep and cattle grazed and rich forests filled with game. Young William loved the country. "The country life is to be preferred," he later said. ". . . it is a sweet and natural retreat from noise and talk, and allows opportunity for reflection."[8]

Sometime after the move from London, probably when William was about five years of age, he began his formal education at the Free Grammar School in Chigwell, about four miles from Wanstead. This school was founded in 1629 by Dr. Samuel Harsnett, the vicar of Chigwell.

As a churchman, Harsnett established rules to guarantee his school's students would not only be educated, but would also be made good Christians. Classes were taught in Latin, Greek, reading, writing, and arithmetic by masters who were instructed to see to it "that the buds of virtue were stirred up" in their students.[9]

"I charge my schoolmasters," Harsnett said, " . . . that they bring up their scholars in the fear of God and reverence toward all men: and that they teach them obedience to their parents, observance to their betters . . . and above all that they chastise them severely for three vices—lying, swearing and filthy speaking."[10] Students who broke the rules, he went on, would be caned by the master.

The lessons William learned at Chigwell stayed with him all his life. As a grown man, he hated those same vices with a passion as great as that of the school's founder. But those weren't the only lessons he learned at the free school. Chigwell made it a practice to enroll a dozen needy students each year and there, for the first time in his life, William, who had spent most of his time alone or with his mother, suddenly met the children of tenant farmers and tradesmen. It was probably at this time that he began to feel the compassion for others that would play a part in so many of the decisions he made in his life.

Life at Chigwell wasn't easy. William and the other students were in class from about daybreak to dusk every day but Sunday, with just a two-hour break each day for lunch and rest. There were only three short holidays each year, at Easter, Pentecost, and Christmas. In class, students learned by repeating the same lessons over and over.

William must have been a good student. He was a serious boy who enjoyed time alone and study. His later writings show that he had a remarkable memory, and we know that by the age of eleven or so he was able to read and write Latin and speak some basic French. While young William was studious and serious, he also enjoyed physical activity, especially foot races against other students. "He was mighty lively, but . . . very early delighted in retirement [solitude]," said John Aubrey, a contemporary of young William's to whom, it is believed, Penn later told his life story.[11]

In those days before there were newspapers, radio or television, preachers in rural churches often read important news from their pulpits on Sunday. So it was that one Sunday in 1652 eight year-old William must have felt very proud as the preacher in the parish church in Chigwell read aloud the news that Admiral Penn had scored a great naval victory over the Dutch fleet.

In honor of this victory, the elder Penn was promoted to General-of-the-Sea, the highest rank possible for a naval officer. In addition, he was rewarded with a gold chain that was hung round his neck by Oliver Cromwell at a banquet at Whitehall, the seat of government in London. More important, he was rewarded with a large estate, known as Macroom, not far from Cork, in Ireland. This estate had once belonged to a Royalist supporter of King Charles, but was taken as punishment once the Civil War ended. Cromwell said the gift of the Irish estate was a reward for the admiral's "good and faithful services performed to the Commonwealth. . . ."[12]

For a time, it must have seemed that the Penn family's future was assured. Admiral Penn was the

wealthy owner of a huge estate. He was a favorite of
Cromwell, the most powerful man in England. He was
still a young man, just thirty-two years of age. His pros-
pects appeared limitless.

This good fortune did not last. In 1654, when William was about ten years old, his father was placed in
command of a fleet that sailed to the West Indies to
capture the Spanish island of Hispaniola. The expedi-
tion failed. Though its failure was not Admiral Penn's
fault, he was blamed. When he returned to London in
1655, he was arrested for failing to carry out his or-
ders. Following a quick trial, Admiral Penn was thrown
into the infamous Tower of London.

This was a particularly difficult time for William.
His father was in jail, perhaps never to be released, for
in those days many men were executed for less cause.
His mother was, no doubt, frightened about the future, particularly since the family now included a daughter, named Margaret but always called Peg, who had
been born in 1652, and a second son, Richard, then an
infant.

William was, by this time, a serious boy who, by his
own admission, spent hours each day reading his Bible,
and meditating until he "was ravished by joy and dis-
solved into tears."[13] In these times of trouble, it was
natural for him to turn even more inward than usual,
to spend more time in prayer and meditation.

One day, at about the time of his father's arrest, he
was alone in his room at Chigwell when he was "suddenly surprised with an inward comfort and . . . an
external glory" that convinced him not only that God
existed but also that he could communicate with Him,
could know His will, and feel His peace. He was also

convinced that he had been "awakened or called upon to a holy life."[14]

In his later life, William Penn would point to this "awakening" as the beginning of his spiritual life. While in the years ahead there would be times when he would seem to turn his back on the belief that he had been chosen by his God to do something special, that belief never left him completely. It remained inside him even as he was tempted by the glory and riches of the world, even as he despaired at the cruelty and hypocrisy he saw all around him. It was like a seed planted in fertile soil. Nourished by knowledge and experience and prayer and the ideas of other men and women he would meet throughout his young manhood, this belief eventually blossomed and changed the world.

Before that happened, though, William Penn had much more to experience and learn. At the age of twelve, he was ready to begin the next great adventure of his life.

TWO

"A Child Alone"

In late 1655, William, his mother, Peg, and the baby Richard moved back to Tower Hill, just a few short steps from the Tower of London where Admiral Penn was imprisoned. Fortunately for the elder Penn, his time behind bars was brief. Cromwell, by then the ruler—or Lord Protector, as he was called—of the British Commonwealth, took pity on the man who had served him so well in the Civil War and ordered him freed. The elder Penn, however, was stripped of his rank and pension, kicked out of the navy he loved, and forced into retirement.

Though William's father would later return to an even higher position in England, he would never again be the same man. The rigors of the campaign in the West Indies, where illness killed thousands of soldiers and sailors, followed by the hardship of his prison stay, left him broken, physically and mentally. The one silver lining in this cloud of trouble was that Cromwell had not stripped him of the Irish estate he'd been given as a reward for his service. In 1656 the Penn family left London for Ireland.

Admiral Sir William Penn

Macroom, the family's new home, was a square, three-story fortress with gray stone battlements. Surrounded by a protective wall, it stood about twenty miles west of the coastal city of Cork, beside a swiftly flowing stream. The castle housed the Penns; their servants, including Anthony, a young West Indian native brought back from the Caribbean by the senior Penn; and a parrot that William's father had brought back from Hispaniola. A small village was nestled outside the castle's walls, populated by Protestant farmers "transplanted" from England to work the thousands of acres that were part of the estate. Though he was without a job in the navy, the senior Penn could easily support his family since the estate provided an income of about three hundred fifty pounds per year, a small fortune in those days.

In Ireland, William had his first real opportunity to get to know his father. Since William was his father's heir, he began learning the business of managing the estate. No doubt the two spent much time together, riding the estate's extensive landholdings, hunting together, or simply talking as fathers and sons do. It was probably at this time, too, that he learned how to use a sword, a requirement for any gentleman in the mid-seventeenth century. At Macroom, a deep and abiding love between the father and son was born. It was a love that would be tested many times in later years.

It was in Ireland, as well, that William saw for the first time the ravages of war, for much of the country and many of its people had been devastated in the years immediately following the end of the Civil War. In those years, Cromwell had turned his attention to subduing the hostile Irish who had dared to support the Royalist side. His army quickly forced the Irish to submit. In the process, much of the country was plundered. Many Irish villages were in ruins. Fully one third of the native population had been killed or maimed in the fighting. Thousands of Catholic survivors, their homes and lands taken by the Protestants who had come to "colonize" the country, wandered the lanes in search of food and shelter. A witness to the devastation said, "The sun never shined, or rather not shined, upon a nation so completely miserable."[1]

The plight of the Irish stirred feelings of pity and compassion in young William, feelings that would resurface throughout his life whenever he encountered suffering. Much later, in a letter to his children in which he advised them to be charitable, he seems to be speaking about some of the things he had seen in those days when he was at Macroom.

> . . . I have often been moved to see very aged and infirm people, but especially poor helpless children, lie all night in bitter weather at the thresholds of Doors in the open streets for want of better lodging. The difference between our condition and theirs has drawn from me . . . great compassion to those poor creatures. Be good to the poor. . . . Be just to them."[2]

Already a serious and sensitive young man, deeply moved by what he saw around him, William continued growing spiritually, experiencing again the closeness with his God that he had first felt in his room at Chigwell. Later in his life, he said that during his time in Ireland, between the ages of twelve and fifteen, "the

Lord visited me . . . and [gave me] divine impressions . . . of Himself. . . ."[3]

In the midst of this time, when William must have been in a particularly receptive frame of mind, he was exposed for the first time to the beliefs of the Christian religious movement known as Quakerism.

The Quaker movement grew out of one man's personal religious experience. That man was George Fox.

The son of a weaver, Fox was born in 1624 in central England. Even as a boy, he spent hours each day in the study of religion. By the age of nineteen, he was disgusted by what he viewed as a huge difference between the way most Christians talked and the way they lived their lives. He became what was known as a "seeker." He traveled the highways and byways of England seeking advice and help from preachers and teachers. Finally, he found the truth he sought in personal revelations he believed came from God. "The Lord did gently lead me along, and did let me see His love, which was endless and eternal . . . ," he later said.[4]

Because of his experiences, Fox believed it was possible for any person to know God as he did—individually and personally. He soon began preaching of what he called "the inward light . . . by which all might know their salvation and their way to God."[5] Those who followed him—and there were many—first called themselves Friends of Truth, the Society of Friends, or, simply, Friends. They got the name "Quakers" after George Fox warned a judge who was about to put him in jail that he should "tremble (or quake) at the word of the Lord."[6] While this name was supposed to be an insult, many Friends soon began calling themselves Quakers.

Quaker beliefs were simple. They believed, for example, that a church was a gathering of people all trying to experience the inner light, not a building made of stone and mortar. They believed that, at their meetings (as their gatherings were called) any Quaker, whether man or woman, could preach the truth, and that it was not necessary to hire or pay clerics. They refused to bear arms because they believed that violence and war were wrong and that men and women were to love one another as they were told to do in the Bible. They refused to swear legal oaths because they believed that a man or woman should always speak the truth and because of what they viewed as a biblical injunction against swearing oaths.

Quakers had other beliefs that many people did not understand. They refused, for example, to take off their hats in the presence of gentry or nobility because they believed all people were equal and that only the Lord deserved special honor. For the same reason, they used what was then known as "familiar" language, saying "thee" and "thou" instead of "you" and "your" to people of a higher social status. While these might seem like small things today, to the English of the seventeenth century they were revolutionary.

Without a formal church structure or paid clerics, the Quaker movement relied on its members to spread its message. Many became itinerant preachers, holding meetings wherever they were invited, preaching on street corners and in open fields, and, on occasion, even interrupting Anglican Church services to spread their own message.

Since the Quakers were different, many people viewed the movement as a threat to the established order and to the Anglican Church. Because of this, Quakers were often persecuted. Still, the movement grew rapidly. It is estimated that in the mid-1600s there were as many as twenty thousand Friends throughout Britain. That number grew to more than fifty thousand by 1700.

By the time the Penn family arrived at Macroom, Quaker meetings were being held in every major city in Ireland, thanks to a steady stream of missionaries sent from England to spread the Quakers' beliefs. In 1657 one of these Quaker missionaries, a man named Thomas Loe, came to Cork.

Loe had become a Friend several years earlier and almost immediately began spreading the word about the young movement. He was, according to those who heard him preach, "a man of an excellent gift, sound, clear and powerful in his ministry."[7]

No doubt the Penns knew of the Quakers before Loe arrived in Ireland, for their strange actions were making them a topic of conversation throughout Britain. Perhaps the elder Penn was simply curious to learn more about this group whose members were willing to face imprisonment and even torture for their faith. Perhaps he was searching for some spiritual answers of his own in the wake of losing his naval command. For whatever reason, when he heard Loe was preaching in nearby Cork, he invited the Quaker to come to Macroom to preach to the household. "Let us . . . hear before we judge," he said.[8]

Since the Friends liked to travel in small groups, Loe probably came to the castle with a group of Friends. Once there, he and his fellow Quakers would have entered with their hats on, despite the fact that "hat honor" would have required them to uncover in the presence of the elder Penn and his family. In sharp contrast to the members and guests of the Penn family, they would have been dressed plainly, in clothing worn by working men and women of the day. Loe would have sat silently for a time before rising to speak, as was the custom at Quaker meetings. When he rose to speak, his words, William Penn later said, had a magical effect on those in the room. While we don't know exactly what he said, there is no doubt he spoke of the Quaker doctrine of "inner light" and of the possibility of direct and mystical communication with the Infinite. As he listened to Loe, thirteen-year-old William must have remembered his own spiritual experience at Chigwell. He must have felt relief to know that he was not the only person to have experienced God's presence so personally and strongly. Suddenly, he heard Anthony, the young servant brought to England from Jamaica, sobbing uncontrollably. Then he turned and saw that his father's face was wet with tears. Moved as much by his father's tears as by Loe's message, he had a sudden vision of a world filled with men and women who believed and acted as these strange, peaceful people did. "What if we should all be Quakers?" he asked himself.[9]

Loe left Macroom and, at least on the surface, life went on as it had before he spoke. Any effect he had on William's father, Anthony, or others who had heard him besides William himself must have been short-lived. For the younger Penn, though, the experience was one he would never forget. ". . .The knowledge of God from the living witness" was with him, he later said, from that day on.[10]

Still, he was not ready, at that time, to join the Quaker movement. For one thing, he was too young to take such a giant step. For another, he questioned his own beliefs, at least from time to time, as almost any sensitive young person would do. In the wake of Loe's visit, he must have spent many hours alone, trying to sort out his feelings. Though he was surrounded by his family, and the castle was often filled with guests, he was very lonely. "I had no relations that inclined to so solitary and spiritual a way," he later wrote. "I was as a child alone."[11]

About a year after Loe's visit, the admiral's exile in Ireland came to an end when, in early September of 1658, Oliver Cromwell died of natural causes.

By that time the English people were heartily sick of what had amounted to a military dictatorship and of years of Puritan piety. One Englishman of the time summed up the general feeling about the Lord Protector's death when he said: "It had pleased God out of His infinite goodness to do that which He would not allow any man the honor of doing."[12]

Almost immediately after Cromwell's death, the English people began grumbling that they wanted a return to the old form of government, a return to a monarchy. The dead king's older son, King Charles II, in exile in Europe with his brothers Henry and James, stood in the wings, ready to make his entrance to center stage.

About a year later, the elder Penn was asked by Parliament to return to England. He and William soon made their way to London and once again took lodgings on Tower Hill. Mrs. Penn and the two younger children stayed in Ireland.

Soon after William and his father returned to London, the elder Penn was invited to sail on a ship that was being sent to bring Charles back to England from his exile. In April 1660, he was aboard the *Naseby* when the as-yet-uncrowned king of England stepped on board in the port of Scheveningen in Holland. One of the king's first official acts was to lay the flat of his sword on the kneeling Penn's shoulder and to pronounce him a Knight of the Realm, Sir William Penn.

On the way back to England, the *Naseby*—named in honor of one of Oliver Cromwell's greatest victories—was rechristened the *Royal Charles*. News of the ship's arrival, with the king on board, proceeded the vessel to Dover, on the coast not far from London. When it docked, one witness wrote, the king was greeted by "a triumph of about 20,000 horses and foots, brandishing their swords and shouting with inexpressible joy; the wayes strew'd with flowers, the bells ringing, the streets hung with tapistry, fountaines running with wine. . . ."[13]

Young William Penn was part of the adoring throng that welcomed the *Royal Charles*. Greeting the newly knighted Sir William, he must have been very proud of the man who was now one of the most influential men in England, as well as a favorite of the king himself.

Sir William, once again in a position of power and prestige, wanted his son to take full advantage of the opportunities that were open to him. It was time, the elder Penn knew, for William the younger to move into the world. In late October 1660 he enrolled his son, then sixteen years of age, as a student at Christ Church College. For young William Penn, the years of his rebellion were about to begin.

THREE

The Formative Years

When young William Penn enrolled at Christ Church College, Oxford, he was, by all indications, destined for great things. Oxford, for years the training ground of the sons of England's aristocrats, was the perfect place for him to learn the social graces that would make him welcome at Court. At Oxford he would also meet other young men who might help him in the future.

The university was a wild, exciting place to be following the return of the monarchy to England. During the years when Charles II was in exile, it had been under Puritan control. In those years, it was a gloomy place, as the Puritans were, for the most part, much more interested in piety than pleasure. In 1660, however, when William became a student, pipe organ music, outlawed under the Puritans, filled the air in the old school's chapels. Students laughed and sang and drank toasts to the king and even cursed on occasion, unlike in the Puritan days when they walked in silence, with their eyes cast devoutly down. And the clothes! Gone were the plain dark pantaloons and jackets of the Puritans, replaced by coats rich with velvet and silk and satin, embroidered waistcoats, lace scarves, breeches with lace at the knee and shoes with fancy silver buckles.

We know little of William's time at Oxford, but he appears to have fit in well, at least at first. He would have had no trouble academically since he had enrolled as a "gentleman scholar," a special type of student that was required to do little more than pay tuition. He certainly would have fit in with the other Cavalier students at the university. He dressed like a Cavalier and was armed with a sword, as were all young men of his class in those days. On his head he wore a long curly wig that, in his case, not only looked fashionable but also hid the fact that he had lost much of his hair as a result of the smallpox he suffered as a boy. As the son of a favorite of the king, his company was probably sought by other young men like himself. And he was, no doubt, popular, since he was later described as a man "of excellent sweetness of disposition, quick of thought and ready utterance."[1]

In April 1661, just a few months after his enrollment, William was invited by his father to watch the parade in honor of the coronation of Charles II as the king of England. William, his father, mother, and young Peg, then about eight years old, joined Samuel Pepys and his wife, and Sir William Batten, a friend of the admiral's, and Mrs. Batten to watch the procession from the windows of a room overlooking the parade route that led from the Tower of London to Whitehall Palace. The king and his brother, James, the duke of York, rode by at the head of a company of men dressed, for some reason, in turbans like Turks, followed by a troop of soldiers dressed in white doublets. "So glorious was the show with gold and silver," Pepys wrote in his diary, "that we were not able to look at it. . . ."[2]

As Charles and James rode past the house where William and the others watched the parade, each in turn greeted the group in the window. William must have been thrilled at the attention paid to his father by the two most powerful men in England. Little did he know, however, how great a part each of these men would play in his life in years to come.

That night the church bells across London rang long and loud in honor of Charles II, some pealing for three hours without stopping. The city's streets were filled with revelers who drank toast after toast to their returned monarch. William surely stayed up late that night, thinking of the wonder of the coronation and, no doubt, made a little dizzy with the knowledge that a world of opportunity lay at his feet.

Soon, though, he was back in Oxford. Sometime after his return to the university, he met Dr. John Owen, a former dean of Christ Church and vice-chancellor of the university. Owen was an independent thinker, a religious nonconformist, and an ardent supporter of Cromwell. After the Royalists returned to power, he—unlike many others—refused to pretend his beliefs had changed. As a result, he was forced from his university posts. Unable to teach, he began holding weekly meetings at his home. At those meetings, he preached his unorthodox views and exhorted students to resist the university's moves to force them to practice the Anglican faith.

In late 1661, William began attending the meetings at Owen's home. Many of the students who attended

Owen's lectures were Puritans. These students were, for the most part, more serious than the Cavaliers that William knew. They were less rowdy, less vain, less prone to the drunkenness and cursing that William had found distasteful ever since his days at Chigwell's public school. While he was not a Puritan, he found the Puritans good company.

At Owen's house William learned that only by asking questions of himself and of others could he ever hope to find the truth. One of the things he began questioning was his own Anglican faith, the faith of his father and the faith that all Oxford students were required to practice. Soon, he joined with other followers of Owen in refusing to attend Anglican services.

Already changed by the feelings of oneness with God he had experienced alone in his room at Chigwell, by his reading and prayer and meditation, and by the joy he had felt when he heard Thomas Loe speak in Ireland, he changed further. He became a religious radical, a nonconformist.

The fact that a number of students—including William—were skipping required religious services was soon noticed by university authorities. The authorities responded by ordering the students to stop visiting Owen's house and to attend services or face fines and reprimands.

To William, this was a moral challenge. To his way of thinking, the university wanted him to turn his back on his own religious beliefs. Certain he was right, he refused to obey. He continued attending the meetings at Owen's house, even though he knew he was putting his future at risk. As he must have known would happen, he was fined and formally reprimanded. There were other punishments, as well, punishments that were meted out by other students, the Cavaliers who hated the Puritans. Later in his life, William wrote that he had suffered "persecution at Oxford," adding that "the Lord sustained me in the midst of that hellish darkness and debauchery."[3]

In addition to fining and reprimanding William, the authorities at Oxford sent a letter to Sir William, advising him of his son's conduct.

The elder Penn, who had sent his son to Oxford to guarantee his future at the Court, was dumbfounded. How could William risk his future over such foolishness? Angry and worried that all his plans for his son could end in disgrace, he ordered William home.

In London, Admiral Penn tried to take William's mind off religion. He saw to it that he enjoyed the city's social scene. While he was home, the two William Penns joined Samuel Pepys for a party following an evening at the theater, and they were all "very merry till late."[4] Undoubtedly, the father and son talked about what happened at Oxford. In any case, William eventually returned to the university. His return lasted only a few weeks, however, before he was dismissed from Christ Church College for good because of his religious nonconformity.

Admiral Penn was outraged. William later said he received "bitter usage" at his father's hands, including "whipping, beating and turning out of doors."[5]

The "turning out of doors" could not have lasted long for he was soon back at home. His relations with his father, however, remained strained. In mid-March 1662, Pepys noted in his diary: "Walking in the garden with Sir W. Penn: his son William is at home, not well. But all things, I fear, do not go well with them—they look discontentedly, but I know not what ails them."[6]

The unsettled and unhappy time in the house on Tower Hill continued for about two months. During that time, the Parliament passed a law known as the Quaker Act, designed "for preventing mischiefs and dangers that may arise by certain persons called Quakers."[7] Among other things, this act made it illegal for five or more Quakers to gather for worship. Those found guilty faced fines, imprisonment, banishment, and sale into slavery.

No doubt the Penns knew of the Quaker Act, though none could have foreseen how it would later be used against young William. In fact, at about that time, Sir William hatched a plan that would, he was sure, take his son's mind off his unhealthy preoccupation with religion. What better solution, he decided, than to send William to Paris, where he could experience pleasure, learn the manners of a gentleman, perhaps even find a young woman who might fill his mind with thoughts that had nothing to do with religion.

Sometime in July, William departed for France. For a time, the admiral's plan worked. In Paris and at the court—then at Fontainebleau, about forty miles from the city—William did, indeed, enjoy the pleasures of the world. He was, after all, a perfectly healthy and normal young man, not quite eighteen years of age. Soon he was dressing in the latest French fashions and, with his natural facility with languages, was speaking French like a native.

His passion for French ways was soon cooled, however. On his way home from the theater late one night, walking along a dark Paris street, he passed a French courtier, probably drunk from a night on the town. The courtier doffed his hat in salute and William, in his own words, "saw him not when he did it." In anger at what he took as a personal slight, the Frenchman drew his sword.

"I will suppose he [might have] killed me for he made several passes at me [with his sword], or I in my defence [might have] killed him," William later wrote.[8] Instead, using skills he learned from his father, he disarmed the French swordsman. According to the law at that time, he could have killed his attacker, but he apologized and let the man go on his way. The episode troubled him deeply, for he knew that the doffing of a man's hat was not worth a life. Suddenly, the splendor of the French court seemed less important. William's preoccupation with religion resurfaced. He was once again the nonconformist who was expelled from Oxford because he followed his beliefs.

"I ask any man of understanding or conscience, if the whole ceremony were worth a man's life?" William wrote of his first experience with nonviolence.[9]

Soon after the duel, he left Paris and traveled to the town of Saumur on the banks of the Loire River. There he attended classes in a Protestant college run by a free-thinking theologian named Moses Amyraut. No doubt William had heard of Amyraut from Owen, for he was one of the most famous thinkers of his time and his beliefs were in line with those of the Oxford nonconformist. He spoke, wrote, and taught about the need for religious tolerance, personal liberty, and nonviolence. He believed in free will and that a man's acts, particularly acts of charity to his fellowman, were the only acts that counted.

William spent about eighteen months at Saumur, attending classes while living in Amyraut's house. Here his religious beliefs began taking firm shape along the lines preached by the theologian. True morality, he came to believe, was expressed in the free acts of a man who was guided by the spirit of God that resides in each person.

William's time in France came to an end in the spring or summer of 1664. At that time, Holland and England were again on the brink of war, and he may have been recalled by his father. He may have decided to leave following Amyraut's death at about that time. In any case, he turned toward home. Before leaving the continent, however, he met yet another man who was to help him formulate the beliefs by which he would live the balance of his life. Algernon Sidney was a freethinker, a political liberal who fled from England when the Royalists returned to power because he was afraid he would be executed as a rebel.

While Owen had talked to William of religious matters, and Amyraut had spoken mainly about social issues, Sidney spoke about government and politics. He was a staunch believer in freedom and the equality of all men. He believed that people have the right to choose their leaders and to remove those leaders from power if they do not live up to their responsibilities. These ideas blended well with the ideas of personal responsibility and freedom that young William had learned from Owen and Amyraut. Slowly, surely, he was formulating a body of beliefs that would guide the rest of his life. These were the same beliefs that would guide him years later when he pieced together the framework of government for the as-yet-undreamed-of province of Pennsylvania.

FOUR

War and Pestilence

William's homecoming in late 1664 was a time of great joy for the entire Penn family. Lady Penn, thirteen-year-old Peg, and Richard, then about ten years of age, had themselves returned to London from Ireland just a short time before William's arrival, so the whole family was together for the first time in four years.

Admiral Penn must have been particularly pleased to see the changes in his elder son. By all accounts, William appeared almost ready to take his place at Court. He dressed in the colorful silks and brocades worn at the Court of King Louis XIV of France. He spoke fluent French. He looked confident and self-possessed. In fact, from what Samuel Pepys said about him, he was a bit too self-confident in those days, and a bit boring, as well, with his constant talk about Paris. "He hath a great deale, if not too much, of the vanity of the French," Pepys wrote in his diary, adding that young William was "affected of speech and gait."[1]

While Pepys thought young Penn had become too much of a dandy, Elizabeth Pepys, his half-French wife, was charmed by William, calling him "a most modish person . . . a fine gentleman."[2]

As far as the admiral was concerned, his plan to take William's mind off religion had worked perfectly. Of course, he needed a little more preparation before he could make himself of service to the king or, for that matter, to the admiral himself. In February 1665, with that end in mind, he enrolled as a student at Lincoln's Inn, one of the four great Inns of Court where young Englishmen of quality went to study law and to mingle with other young men destined for government service. There, Admiral Penn hoped, his son would get the training he needed to become a lawyer for the Crown and to help manage the Penn family's extensive estates.

Lincoln's Inn was then more a place where young gentlemen went to socialize than a law school. Students were only required to be in residence at the college for about four months out of the year, and even then they were not required to do much work. Most student activity centered around the school's Old Hall. Built at the end of the fifteenth century, this was a stone-walled, castlelike building with stained-glass windows and oak-paneled walls. Its wooden floor was covered with straw, and in its center a huge fire burned, sending its smoke curling up thirty feet to where it escaped through vents placed beneath the ceiling. Here students gathered to dine at long tables, to watch plays and entertainments, and, when there were no parties to attend, to talk about the law. William, who enjoyed a good meal as much as any man, must have loved dining in the Old Hall, since each student's daily meal ration included six pounds of prime roast beef.

Young William hardly had time to get used to his new surroundings at the Inn before the expected war between the Dutch and English began. Sir William was made captain of the *Royal Charles*, the same great ship of war that had carried Charles II back to England at the end of his exile. He was, at the same time, given the title Great Captain Commander and was placed in command of a squadron of thirty-eight ships of war.

The elder Penn saw his new command as an opportunity to have his son meet important people, including James, the duke of York, who was in overall command of the war fleet and who would be on board the *Royal Charles* in his role as Lord High Admiral of the Royal Navy. Consequently, in early April, just a few weeks after William had enrolled at Lincoln's Inn, Admiral Penn ordered him to leave school and to join him as an unofficial aide.

For several weeks, William was at his father's side as the admiral prepared his men and ships to sail off to war. During that time, he gained a new appreciation of his father as a man capable of leading others into battle. It is likely that he asked his father for permission to sail into battle aboard the *Royal Charles*. The elder Penn, however, would not have wanted to put his son in harm's way. Instead, in late April, not long before the fleet sailed, he sent William ashore with dispatches addressed to the king.

On April 23, after William landed at Harwich, a port city not far from London, he wrote a letter filled with love and concern to his father. "I pray God," he said, " . . . that you come home secure . . . [and that] he will cover your head in that smoky day. As I never knew what a father was till I had wisdom enough to prize him, so can I safely say, that now, of all time, your concerns are most dear to me. It is hard, meantime to lose both a father and a friend."[3]

After seeing to it that his letter would be delivered to the flagship, William traveled by carriage to London, arriving at about dawn the next day.

Charles II, still in bed when William arrived at Whitehall Palace on the banks of the Thames, was wakened with the news that a messenger had arrived with word from the fleet. If, as was likely, it had been Admiral Penn's intention for his son to meet the king informally, his plan worked to perfection, for, William later said, Charles jumped from his bed and ran to meet him dressed "only in his gown and slippers."[4]

The king and William spoke together for about thirty minutes, a private conversation that ensured the king would long remember the admiral's son. Later, William recounted that conversation in a second letter to his father. When Charles II saw him, he told Sir William: "He asked how you [were] several times . . . [then] bid me go about your business and mine too." In this letter, William's concern for his father is again apparent. "I pray God be with you, and be your armour in the day of controversy!" he wrote.[5]

Following this stint of what must have been exciting duty, William returned to Lincoln's Inn, though with his father at war, he must have been distracted. There was soon, however, more than the war to distract him.

To get to the college each day, William walked from Tower Hill across the city, past St. Paul's Cathedral, down Ludgate Street and then along Fleet Street, today famous as the center of the newspaper publishing industry in London. On his walk, he passed the Old

Bailey, the famous courthouse, and Newgate Prison, and the old city gate known as the Temple Bar. As he walked, he would have seen firsthand the results of the government's recent decision to strictly enforce a set of laws known as the Clarendon Code. These laws made it a crime for any English citizen to practice any faith other then Anglicanism. Lawbreakers, including women and children, were arrested, heavily fined, or brutally tortured. He could not have helped but notice that many of those being punished were Quakers. Seeing what he saw each day turned his thoughts away from fancy clothes and military matters and the other things he had been interested in since his return from France. Once again, he began to withdraw into himself, to turn his back on the world.

During those months, a catastrophe was brewing in one of the slum neighborhoods outside the city proper. The first sign of the pending disaster was the report, in early December, of a case of the plague in one of the areas populated by beggars and nearly destitute peddlers. It wasn't unusual for scattered cases of the disease known as the Black Death to be reported, so few Londoners took notice. For a time, the cold winter weather held the disease in check. Then, as temperatures began warming, one person, then two, then scores fell sick.

At first, the disease that ravaged London about once every generation was largely concentrated in the city's poorest and most crowded areas, away from Tower Hill, far from Lincoln's Inn. Within weeks, though, it spread inside the city gates.

On June 3, the very day the English fleet under the joint command of Admiral Penn and the duke of York engaged the Dutch in a great sea battle off the coast of

Holland, Samuel Pepys said he saw the first signs of the plague in the city itself. "This day . . . I did in Drury Lane see two or three houses marked with a red cross upon the doors, and 'Lord have mercy on us' writ there . . . ," he wrote in his diary.[6]

Like Pepys, William undoubtedly saw the red crosses and scrawled prayers that marked the houses of the infected who were forced to quarantine themselves, without medical care and often without food or water. He saw diseased rats writhing in the gutters and heard the cries of "Bring out your dead!" as wagons trundled along the cobblestone streets each morning to be loaded with the corpses of those who died during the night. He heard the church bells tolling on and on in sadness; and no doubt he heard the old nursery rhyme about the plague:

> *Ring-a-ring o'roses,*
> *A pocketful of posies,*
> *A'tishoo, a'tishoo,*
> *We all fall down.*

With that nursery rhyme in mind, he frequently checked his skin for any sign of the red rash—the "ring o'roses"—that was the first symptom of the deadly disease. And like most in the city, he carried a "pocketful of posies" to sniff as a guard against infection, and prayed that he wouldn't be one of the thousands who sneezed and then fell down sick.

By the middle of July, two thousand Londoners were dying of the plague each week. "The Sickenesse is got into our parish this week; and is indeed everywhere," Pepys wrote that month.[7] He was correct. It was everywhere. More than thirty thousand people died in August, so many that they had to be buried in huge communal graves outside the city walls. "But Lord," Pepys wrote in that month, "how sad a sight it is to see the streets empty of people. . . ."[8]

No one in the Penn family died in the epidemic, but William was deeply moved by the death and suffering he saw all around. At the same time, he saw orthodox ministers in London flee from their churches, leaving sick and suffering parishioners behind. And he watched as Quakers, seeming not to care about their own health, ministered to the sick, entered the houses of the dying where no one else would go, brought food and water to prisoners in the city's jails where the plague raged unchecked.

William was disappointed by the way many ministers of the Anglican Church and other established religions acted during the plague. Like George Fox before him, he saw that many ministers preached a faith they did not practice. Later, he wrote, "In the time of the Great Plague in London, [the Lord] gave me deep sense . . . of the vanity of this world, of the irreligiousness of the religious in it." At that time, he thought seriously of turning his back on those religions for he said he "made mournful and bitter cries to [God] that He would show me His own way of life and salvation."[9]

By October, when William celebrated his twenty-first birthday, the plague had run its course in London. It had killed about seventy thousand people, or one of every seven city residents.

At about that time, Admiral Penn came home from the war. This time, though the English had beaten the Dutch, there was no hero's welcome awaiting Sir William. London was still reeling from the plague, and the

The Diseases and Casualties this Week.

Abortive	4
Aged	45
Bleeding	1
Broken legge	1
Broke her scull by a fall in the streer at St. Mary VVoolchurch	1
Childbed	28
Chrisomes	9
Consumption	126
Convulsion	89
Cough	1
Dropsie	53
Feaver	348
Flox and Small-pox	11
Flux	1
Frighted	2
Gowt	1
Grief	3
Griping in the Guts	79
Head-mould-shot	1
Jaundies	7

Imposthume	18
Infants	22
Kingsevil	4
Lethargy	1
Livergrown	1
Meagrome	1
Palsie	1
Plague	4237
Purples	2
Quinsie	5
Rickets	23
Rising of the Lights	18
Rupture	1
Scurvy	3
Shingles	1
Spotted Feaver	166
Stilborn	4
Stone	2
Stopping of the stomach	17
Strangury	3
Suddenly	2
Surfeit	74
Teeth	111
Thrush	6
Tissick	9
Ulcer	1
Vomiting	10
Winde	4
Wormes	20

Christned { Males — 90 / Females — 81 / In all — 171 } Buried { Males — 2777 / Females — 2791 / In all — 5568 } Plague — 4237

Increased in the Burials this Week — 249

Parishes clear of the Plague — 27 Parishes Infected — 103

The Assize of Bread set forth by Order of the Lord Maior and Court of Aldermen, A penny Wheaten Loaf to contain Nine Ounces and a half, and three half-penny White Loaves the like weight.

This Bill of Mortality for the week of August 15–22, 1665, records 4,237 people dead of the plague. The month of August was the height of the epidemic.

naval victory seemed empty to the thousands who had lost loved ones and friends to the deadly disease.

The elder Penn, meanwhile, was shocked to see that William was once again turning his back on the world. He knew he had to do something to take his son's mind off religious matters. William, the admiral decided, would go to Ireland. Macroom, the estate awarded to Sir William by Cromwell, had been taken back by the king and returned to its original owner. In its place Admiral Penn had been given Shanagarry Castle, an even larger estate near the port city of Cork. Since William was now an adult, he could handle the transfer of the properties. In that way, he would also be kept too busy to mope about religion.

In January 1666, William crossed the Irish Sea to Cork. In addition to taking care of his father's business affairs, he visited the court of the duke of Ormonde, the king's representative in Ireland. As the son of Admiral Sir William Penn, he was welcome to enjoy the active social life at the Court in Dublin.

At about this time, an English army garrison at the town of Carrickfergus mutinied. The duke of Ormonde's son, the earl of Arran, was sent to suppress them. William, perhaps to prove to himself that he was as brave a soldier as his father, went with Arran as a "gentleman volunteer." The mutiny was quickly put down with a brief assault in which William proved to be a brave, skilled soldier. In fact, the duke of Ormonde was so impressed that he wrote to the admiral saying that William should become a professional soldier. At the same time, William wrote to his father asking for permission to assume the command of a company of infantry. The elder Penn, after a life of command, must have known his son was not cut out to spend his life as a soldier. On July 17, 1666, he wrote a cautionary letter to William. "I [hope] your youthful desires [don't] outrun your discretion," he said.[10]

The social life at Court and the romance of soldiering had turned William's head once again and for a time at least the strong religious feelings he had in London during the plague faded. William himself later said that at this time of his life, "the glory of the world overtook me, and I was even ready to give up myself unto it. . . ."[11]

It was at about this time that a famous portrait of William Penn was painted. Known as the "armor portrait," it portrays the future Quaker wearing a soldier's armor, with a white scarf at his neck. There is no hint that the young man in the portrait, obviously proud of his soldierly exploits, had ever entertained thoughts of nonviolence. There's surely no hint that William Penn was about to turn his back on what he called the glory of the world once and for all.

Considered the most accurate image
of William Penn, this "Armor Portrait"
was painted in October of 1666 when
Penn was twenty-two years old.

FIVE

Convincement

In the fall of 1666, William left Dublin and the excitement of Court and made his way to Shanagarry Castle. The estate's holdings included about eight square miles of land overlooking Cork harbor and the Atlantic Ocean at the southernmost tip of Ireland. There, he was kept busy taking care of legal affairs surrounding Admiral Penn's ownership of the Shanagarry estate. Though William had spent just a brief time as a law student at Lincoln's Inn, he apparently learned some law, for he quickly resolved most of the claims against the admiral's ownership of the land and castle.

With most of the legal matters solved, he was enjoying his life as lord of the manor in Ireland when, in the fall of 1666, he received word that London, still reeling from the effects of the plague, had been ravaged by a fire that almost destroyed the city.

The Great Fire of London, as it has come to be called, started at three o'clock in the morning on September 2 in a baker's house on Pudding Lane not far from London Bridge. Spreading from the baker's house,

This picture, drawn by an unknown artist after the Great Fire in 1666, shows how easily the fire raged out of control, jumping from one wooden structure to the next.

the fire soon engulfed nearby homes and shops. By dawn, three hundred houses and the ancient wooden bridge itself were on fire.

Fires were commonplace in London in the mid-seventeenth century and, at first, most of the city's residents were unconcerned. Soon, though, panic set in as an unusually strong wind fed flames that leapt from one wooden building to another. By the fire's second day, it had spread along the banks of the Thames River,

where tongues of flame ignited warehouses and cellars filled with tallow, oil, timber, and coal. At the same time, the strong wind carried sparks and burning embers to set new fires away from the main blaze. "With one's face in the wind," Pepys wrote in his diary, "you were almost burned with a shower of fire drops."[1] During the next three days almost half of London was destroyed. Only eight people died in the fire, but more than thirteen thousand dwellings were destroyed. Tens of thousands of Londoners were left homeless, forced to live in tents on the outskirts of the gutted city.

Luckily for the Penns, while the fire threatened Tower Hill, their house was spared. There was no reason, at that time, for William to return home. About five months later, however, he was called home by his father who wanted to talk with him about the management of the Irish estate. He sailed for England sometime in early February and arrived in time to take part in fifteen-year-old Peg's marriage to a twenty-four-year-old businessman named Anthony Lowther.

William's homecoming was not as joyous as it might have been. Much of the city of London was in ruins. Some cellars in the city still smoldered. Homeless men, women, and children shivered in tents and makeshift dwellings in the midst of a bitterly cold winter.

All was not well in the house on Tower Hill, either. Sir William was suffering terribly from gout, a painful disease that causes swelling in the feet and ankles and makes walking almost impossible. At the same time, he was under attack by political enemies. Though the admiral's fleet had defeated the Dutch in the sea battle fought about a year earlier, the English at that time had not pressed their advantage and destroyed the Dutch fleet. As the war with Holland continued, many in England wrongly blamed the elder Penn for not sending all the Dutch ships to the bottom when he had the chance, even though the decision had not been his to make. If all that wasn't bad enough, he'd been retired from active sea duty by the duke of York, transferred to a desk job at the navy office on Tower Hill. Disappointed, bitter, in physical pain, and away from the sea he loved, the admiral spent many hours sitting with his afflicted foot propped on a stool, drinking sack, a dry, white wine that was his favorite beverage.

With the admiral mired in his own troubles and London in ruins and filled with suffering people, Peg's wedding was a rather somber affair. The ceremony, held on Valentine's Day, was attended only by family members and a few friends. The wedding dinner was simple, served on plates borrowed from Pepys, who complained in his diary about what he called the "shameful meanness" (stinginess) of the admiral for not hosting a bigger party with more food and drink.[2]

All in all, William could not have been very happy at home. The closeness he and his father had shared on the *Royal Charles* was gone. The suffering he saw all around and the sadness he saw in his father, an old man before his time, must have made him painfully aware of the fleeting nature of fame and power and, indeed, of life itself. In that frame of mind, he must have been happy when the time came for him to return to Ireland just a few weeks after his sister's wedding.

Often, in the lives of many men and women, great events happen as the result of seemingly small decisions. In the summer of 1667, not long after his return to Shanagarry, William Penn made such a small decision. He decided to visit the nearby city of Cork and, while there, to purchase some clothing at a shop owned by a Quaker woman. As he rode his horse from the estate to the city, dressed in his finery, with his fancy wig in place and his sword strapped to his waist, he had no plans other than to add to his wardrobe. As he rode across one of the drawbridges that led to the old walled city where it nestled on an island in the River

Lee, he surely had no idea that his life was about to change, for good and always.

William had been to the Quaker woman's shop years before, when the Penn family lived at Macroom. As soon as he entered her shop he recognized her in her plain clothing and the close-fitting cap called a "pinner" worn by many women in those days. Forgetting that he had grown from boyhood to manhood since the last time she had seen him, William was surprised when she did not recognize him as well. As soon as he introduced himself, however, she remembered the son of Admiral Penn. Suddenly, talking to the Quaker woman, William remembered the day, years before, when Thomas Loe had spoken at the manor house. As he recalled Loe's visit to Macroom, some of the warmth and wonder he felt when he had heard the Quaker's words a decade earlier were rekindled in his heart. Excited, he began speaking of that day. If he knew where Loe was, he said, he would go to hear him speak again, even if it meant riding his horse one hundred miles.

There was no need to ride one hundred miles, the woman said, or even ten, for at that moment Loe was in Cork and would be speaking at a Quaker meeting the very next day.

William spent that night in Cork, perhaps with a family of Friends, perhaps in one of the city's inns. Wherever he spent the night, he must have been filled with a mixture of joy and apprehension. Always thoughtful and reflective, he must have thought back to the revelation he had had in his room at Chigwell and remembered how that experience was given meaning by Loe's sermon at Macroom. He must have recalled his time at Oxford and all he had learned about man's relationship with God from Dr. Owen. He certainly thought again of Moses Amyraut, his teacher in France. He must have recalled, as well, how he had been attracted again and again by the world's glory, how he had turned his back on his religious longings to embrace power and fashion and prestige. Perhaps that night he had an idea that his time of uncertainty was about to end. But which path would he follow? Would he, once and for all, embrace the world of glory? Or would he finally embrace a life dedicated only to his God?

The next day, William made his way to the Quaker home where the meeting was to be held. He entered and took a seat. Dressed in his fancy clothing, surrounded by the plainly dressed Quakers, Penn might have felt out of place, but the Friends would have nodded and smiled and made him feel welcome, for that was their way. Eagerly, William searched the crowd for some sign of Thomas Loe. Finally, he spied him seated among a group of elders at the front of the meeting room. He looked gray, drawn and tired. Ten years of traveling in the Quaker cause, years in which he spent months in Irish and English prisons, often brutally treated for his faith, had made him look much older than his thirty-five years. For a time, Loe did not speak. Finally, he stood.

"There is a Faith," he said, "there is a Faith that overcometh the world, and there is a Faith that is overcome by the world."[3]

As soon as William Penn the younger heard those words, he knew he had found the answer he had been seeking. He knew, in his heart, that his time of hesitation was at an end. He had had faith, he knew, but it was a faith that was all too easily overcome by the world. No longer could he serve two masters. The world represented by his father and the king and his court must be given up once and for all. As his father and the black servant, Anthony, had done ten years earlier when they heard Loe's words at Macroom, "he wept much."[4] It seemed to him, he later said, "as if a Voice said, 'Stand on thy feet! How dost thou know but somebody may be reached by thy tears.'" He stood in silent witness to his acceptance of the Quaker beliefs.[5]

After that meeting, William and Loe went to a nearby Friend's house where they spoke more about Quaker beliefs. As their discussion ended, Loe said he was in need of a horse to take him to the next stop on his journey. His own, he explained, was worn out. Without hesitation, William offered his horse, a fine mount he had brought from France, to the Quaker preacher. Loe refused his offer. William was stung by Loe's refusal, believing he "was not yet enough of a Quaker" to make his gift acceptable.[6]

In one regard, William was much like his father. He was a man of action. If he was not enough of a Quaker, he would become one. For the next few weeks, he attended one Quaker meeting after another. He did not, however, immediately begin acting like a Friend. He did not change his fancy dress. He wore his wig and continued wearing his sword, even though the Quakers were nonviolent. He did not immediately begin speaking like a Quaker, using "thee" and "thou." Though he was ready to accept Quaker beliefs, he was not yet ready, in those very early days, to accept the scorn that was sure to be heaped on him if he acted like a Quaker in public.

That came to an end on September 3, 1667, just a few weeks after William experienced what he called his Quaker "convincement." On that day, he attended a meeting in Cork. As usual, the Quakers in the house were dressed in the plain clothes they favored. William wore his ruffled shirt and fancy breeches, silk vest and coat. His wig was in place and his sword was at his waist.

As the meeting started, he and the others sat in silent meditation. Suddenly, the quiet in the room was shattered when an English soldier burst into the room. In those days, non-Quakers often came to meetings just to cause trouble.

William was angered and insulted by the soldier's actions. He jumped to his feet, grabbed the soldier's collar, and started toward a flight of stairs, intending, no doubt, to throw him down the steps. Friends in the room hurried to stop him, to remind him that retaliation and violence were not their way.

William immediately realized they were right. Not only did his actions violate Quaker beliefs, but they also were dangerous. Throwing the soldier bodily from the meeting, as he wanted to do, would almost certainly bring constables running, more than happy to arrest the Quakers. He let the soldier go.

The constables came in any event, undoubtedly hailed by the soldier. William and eighteen of the Friends at the meeting were arrested.

The nineteen were quickly hauled into court. There the mayor of Cork, Christopher Rye, acted as judge. He recognized William as Admiral Penn's son. Why, the judge wondered, is a gentlemen like you keeping company with these despised Quakers? Surely this is some sort of mistake. You cannot be one of them. He offered the new Quaker convert a chance to go free on bond.

William refused the judge's offer. "Whether you think it or not," he said, "I am a Quaker and if you send my friends to jail, I am willing to go with them."[7]

With those words he publicly announced for the first time that he was a Quaker. For the first time he proved that he was willing to accept scorn and punishment because of his beliefs. And his punishment was not long in coming. Immediately, the judge ordered William and his companions thrown in jail.

As a gentleman, William was allowed to keep his sword even as he was being led to jail. According to a story that may be more fiction than fact, he unstrapped his sword just before he stepped across the threshold into the Cork city prison. Bowing, he handed it to a passerby with the promise that from that day forward he would walk unarmed in an armed world.

Whether that story is factual or simply a legend like those that seem to grow around all famous men and women, the fact remains that William Penn the younger was from that day forward fully committed to his life as a Quaker. His time of indecision was at an end. The rebellious streak that had caused him to be expelled from Oxford, that led him to turn his back on the glory of the world that was rightly his, that compelled him to seek God in nonconformity, had finally led him to a faith that would be both his burden and his great glory.

SIX

⌒⌒⌒⌒⌒

Commitments

While young William Penn was ready to suffer for his beliefs, he was not about to submit quietly to what he viewed as injustice. Soon after the prison gates swung shut behind him, he wrote to Lord Orrery, a longtime friend of his father's and the most powerful Englishman in Ireland. In his letter, he argued that the imprisonment of the Quakers was unjust, since the law used to punish him and the other Friends had been written to protect the Crown against traitors, not peaceful people who gathered to praise God. He went on to remind Orrery that there was no better way to "improve or advantage" a country than to see to it that all people enjoyed "freedom in things relating to conscience."[1]

Luckily for William and seventeen of his companions, the persuasive argument he used in his letter to Orrery worked. They were soon released. Richard Pike, one of the Quakers locked up with William, however, was not so fortunate. Pike died of "cold and distemper, contracted in the gaol."[2] Indeed, it is surprising that only one died. Like all jails in those days, Cork's was dark, dank, filthy, and disease-ridden; not much better than a cesspool. Its prisoners were regularly beaten or starved unless they had money to bribe their keepers.

On October 12, 1667, not long after William's release, his father wrote a letter to his son in Ireland. "By this [letter]," his father wrote, "I . . . command that you come to me with all possible speed. . . ."[3] William knew as soon as he read those words that Orrery or one of his father's other friends in Ireland had written to the admiral telling him of his son's arrest. He chose to ignore that letter. He could not ignore a second, more demanding message, sent just a few days later. " . . . I charge you to repair to me with all possible speed . . . and not to make any stay there, or any place upon your road, until it pleases God you see me. . . ."[4]

Though William was a young man now, no longer a boy, he must have felt like a child who was about to be punished as he thought of going home to face his father. He asked another Quaker, forty-year-old Josiah Coale, to accompany him to England. Coale, like William, came from a highborn family, and William may have hoped that when his father saw his son in the company of another gentleman Quaker, he might be less angry.

While William was in Ireland, the Penn family had moved to a new, fine house in Wanstead, not far from London. In December, after a brief stop in Bristol where the two Quakers attended a meeting, they made their way to the manor. In Coale's presence, the admiral held his temper, even though the two younger men kept their hats on and spoke in the Quaker way. Soon, though, the two William Penns were alone. The admiral angrily questioned his son. How dare he not pay hat honor to his father? How dare he use *thee* and *thou* when speaking to his betters? Didn't he realize how this behavior could damage his place in society? How it could destroy his future?

It was not disrespect, William answered, since, in the eyes of God and the Quakers, all men were equal and no one man should be given respect that wasn't given to all men.

Though it went against everything the admiral believed, he was willing to compromise. *Thee* and *thou* whomever you wish, he said, except for the king, the duke of York, and himself. Remove your hat to no man, he said, except the same three: King Charles II, his brother James, and the admiral himself. Surely William could bend that much?

William refused to budge. He was sorry, he told his father, but it was a matter of conscience.

At his son's refusal, the admiral was so angry that he could not trust himself to speak. He sent William to his room and told him to be ready to go out with him early the next morning.

The next morning, the father and son rode in the admiral's coach to a nearby tavern where they could speak without fear of being overheard by servants. They made their way to a private room. The admiral closed the door. His voice shaking, he told William he was going to pray that he would be saved from the clutches of Quakerism.

To William, this was blasphemy. He rushed across the room, threw open a window, and cried that he would throw himself to the stones below before he let his father say such a terrible prayer.

Luckily for both William and his father, they were interrupted by a knock at the tavern door. A friend of the admiral's, seeing his coach below, had stopped to say hello. The interruption gave the two William Penns a chance to calm down and ended the nasty scene. It must have been like rubbing salt in the elder Penn's wounds, however, when the friend congratulated him on having such a fine, upstanding son.

After that, William and his father managed to maintain an uneasy peace in the big house in Wanstead. Sir William was kept busy with his duties at the navy office and with the ongoing war with Holland. William must have taken pains to stay out of his father's way. It was a sad time for both men. Pepys, in his diary, noted that "Mr. William Penn, who is lately come over from Ireland, is a Quaker . . . or some very melancholy thing . . . [he] cares for no company. . . ."[5]

William, meanwhile, continued his Quaker activities. Then, in the late spring of 1668, he was again arrested for violating the law that made it illegal for more than five Quakers to gather. Though he was soon freed by a magistrate who recognized him, his father learned of the arrest.

By this time, the admiral was in poor health. He was, in addition, under attack at the navy department where old—and false—charges that he stole prize goods for his own use during his service had resurfaced. When he learned that William was again in trouble, he was in no mood for what he considered his son's foolishness. He ordered William home.

William obeyed his father's command. On his way home, however, he went to a Quaker meeting and visited the home of a Friend. While he was there, a beautiful young woman entered the room. Her name, he learned, was Gulielma Maria Springett.

Twenty-four-year-old Guli, as she was called, was the daughter of Mary Springett and the stepdaughter of Isaac Penington, both active Quakers. She herself was a convinced Friend. William lost his heart to her immediately. Perhaps he was stricken by her looks, of which her friend Thomas Ellwood had once said "wanted nothing to render her completely Comely," or by her habitual kindness, which Ellwood described as "springing from the abundant Affability, Courtesy and Sweetness of her natural Temper."[6]

Reluctantly, William left Guli and made his way to Wanstead. There, the admiral was no longer willing to compromise. He was also no longer willing to stand by as his son destroyed not just himself but the rest of his family because of his beliefs. He told William to pack his things and leave. Furthermore, Sir William said, the inheritance that would have been his son's would be given to someone "that pleased him better."[7]

Where William went or how he lived without funds after his father ordered him to leave is not known. No doubt, Friends took care of him, and his mother slipped him some money from time to time. However he managed to live, he was free, now, to devote himself even more fully to the Quaker cause. Immediately, he became one of the most active Friends in England. He preached in public, debated conformist preachers who spoke out against the Friends, and wrote a religious tract, *The Truth Exalted*, that explained the Quaker way of life. This was to be just the first of dozens of such tracts he would publish during his life.

Because of his position as the admiral's son, William had access to the Court and to high-ranking government officials. As a Quaker Cavalier, he was the only link the movement had with those in power. He made use of his position, visiting several of the most powerful men in the kingdom to argue that the persecution of the Friends was illegal and immoral.

At about this time, Thomas Loe died. He was old before his time, worn out by his travels, frequent imprisonment, and beatings and starvation at the hands of his jailers. William was in the room as his mentor spoke his last words. "Bear thy Cross," he said, " . . . , and God will give thee an eternal Crown of Glory."

On the day Loe was buried, Penn wrote to another Friend that Loe was a man "Whom my soul loved, while alive, and honors now dead."[8]

Not long after Loe's death, William, filled with Quaker zeal as a new convert, published a pamphlet titled *The Sandy Foundation Shaken*. Some of what he said seemed to challenge basic Christian doctrine. As such, it could be viewed as an attack on the Anglican Church, and, by extension, on the Crown.

This pamphlet attracted the attention of the Anglican Bishop of London, who had the authority to imprison anyone he thought was guilty of heresy. On December 12, 1668, William was again arrested. This time, though, he was in serious trouble, which would not go away just because he was Sir William's son. He was thrown into the Tower of London, where his father had been imprisoned when William was a boy.

The Tower of London is not really a tower. It is a formidable castle built on a hill at the foot of London Bridge. Properly called the Royal Palace and Fortress of the Tower of London, it stands over the old city of London like a hulking, silent watchman. The first Tower was a wooden structure built by William the Conqueror in 1067. Within a decade, construction began on a larger fortress with massive stone walls topped by four turrets—three square and one rounded. That fortress, known as the White Tower, was completed in about 1100. Eventually, that main building was surrounded by a complex of gateways, outbuildings, additional towers, and protective bastions.

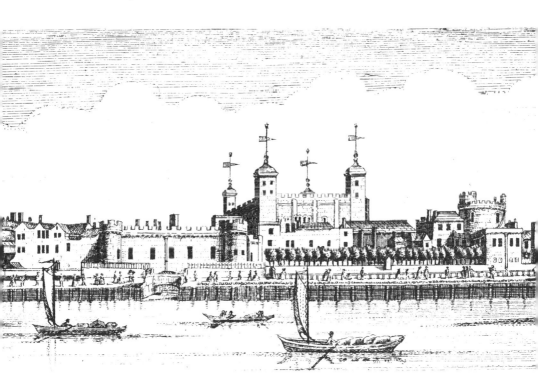

The Tower of London as seen from across the River Thames

At first, William was held in relative comfort in an area of the fortress where the Tower's chief constable resided. Soon, though, he was moved to a tiny cell high under the roof of one of the towers. Though William could have gained his freedom at any time by recanting, or taking back what he had written, he refused. For eight months he was held prisoner. His cell froze in winter and was like an oven under the summer sun. Much of the sparse hair that had grown back after his bout with smallpox fell out, probably because of a poor diet. He was allowed almost no communication with the outside world, though a servant, Francis Cooke, was able to visit on the day before Christmas. Cooke brought a message from the bishop. "Recant . . . at an appointed time before . . . all the city or else be a prisoner during [your] life," the bishop said.[9]

Penn refused. "Thou mayst tell my father, whom I know will ask thee," he told Cooke, " . . . that my prison shall be my grave before I will budge [an inch], for I owe my conscience to no mortal man. . . ."[10]

Though William was held under close guard, he was allowed the freedom to write. He took advantage of this opportunity to write yet another pamphlet. He took as its title Thomas Loe's dying words. *No Cross, No Crown* explained the Quaker beliefs in detail.

During this period, Josiah Coale, the Friend who had accompanied William to Wanstead, died at the age of about forty-four. In the space of just a few months, both Loe and Coale had died. "My soul is often heavy and bowed down in the sense of the loss of these valiants," William said upon learning of Coale's death.[11]

While William was in the Tower, Admiral Penn apparently never wrote to him and certainly never visited. He did, however, begin to feel glimmerings of respect for his son for standing up for his beliefs. On January 20, 1669, the elder Penn wrote a new will, bequeathing to his son the gold chain and medal he had received from Oliver Cromwell in recognition of his service during the Civil War. In addition, he stated that William was to receive most of his estate. The period of estrangement between father and son, it appeared, was nearing its end.

Meanwhile, events were transpiring that would make it possible for William to avoid dying in the Tower. The king, no doubt because of his friendship with Sir William, sent his own chaplain, Dr. Edward Stillingfleet, to visit William in his cell and to question him in hopes that William could clarify his statements and win his release. At first, things did not go well. William told Stillingfleet to tell the king that he would never be forced to change his beliefs. " . . . [T]he Tower is the Worst argument in the world to convince me," he said.[12] Force, he added, may make a man a hypocrite, it will never make him a convert.

Gradually, though, the king's chaplain was able to convince William to write yet another pamphlet, explaining more clearly what he had meant in *The Sandy Foundation Shaken*. William set to work and quickly completed a tract in which he made it plain that he had not meant to attack the beliefs of the Anglican Church.

Upon reading that pamphlet, Stillingfleet was satisfied that William's beliefs were not blasphemous. King Charles agreed and, on July 28, 1669, he signed the order to set William free.

William had been in prison for almost nine months. He was weak and tired and now almost completely bald as he walked through the gate of the old fortress. Weak and tired as he was, however, he could take comfort in the knowledge that he had stood by his new faith and passed a true test of his convincement. Without bending his principles, he had gained the freedom to continue fighting for rights for the Quakers and other nonconformists.

SEVEN

"Against the Peace of the King…"

In mid-September 1669, about six weeks after William was released from the Tower of London, his father sent him to Ireland, to the Shanagarry estate. Though the admiral was beginning to respect his son's courage and willingness to suffer for his beliefs, he wanted William to avoid further difficulties with the law. In Ireland, the elder Penn hoped, his son would be too busy to cause trouble.

William, no doubt, was looking forward to returning to Shanagarry, where he was the lord of the manor. Before he departed, though, William had one important stop to make. On his way to the port of Bristol, he left the main road and rode north to the village of Amersham, where Guli Springett lived with her mother and stepfather.

William and Guli had written to each other regularly since their first meeting. They had grown close through their letters. Now he wanted to see her again, even if it meant that his father's business would have to wait for a time.

At first, William planned to visit Guli and her family for just one day. Once he was with her again, however, he found one excuse after another to delay his departure. The young couple went to meetings together, they walked together in the woods near Amersham, they talked of the future. By the time William finally managed to tear himself away, five days later, they had an understanding that someday they would marry.

At about this time, William hired a Quaker named Philip Ford to manage his business affairs. He probably hired Ford because he felt sorry for him. An unsuccessful shopkeeper who had suffered because of his Quaker beliefs, Ford was selling shoelaces on the streets of London not long before he became William's business manager. From the beginning of their relationship, Penn trusted Ford completely. It was a trust that would cost him dearly.

The two men traveled together to Bristol, arriving in late September. From there, Ford went on to Ireland while Penn visited George Fox, the Quaker founder. It is likely the two Quakers had met earlier, but their acquaintance grew into friendship as Penn delayed his sailing for a month. At that time, Fox was about to marry Margaret Fell, a Quaker leader herself and one of the most famous Friends of her time. As was the custom, Fox and the widow Fell went before a meeting to get formal approval of their planned marriage. At that meeting, William spoke in favor of Fox's proposed marriage.

Finally, on October 23, he departed for Ireland, arriving three days later. Almost immediately, he discovered that many Irish Quakers were imprisoned. "I found [the Quakers] of that Kingdom under too general per-

Gulielma Maria Springett

secution, and those of the City of Cork almost all in Prison," he wrote.[1]

Knowing from his own experience what imprisonment was like, he began visiting Friends being held in Cork's jail. He found eighty Quakers locked in one tiny enclosure, without adequate food or water. Men, women, and children were forced to sleep in tiny, cavelike holes chopped in the stone walls of their cells. Many, including children, were held in stocks, unable to move, in excruciating pain.

Immediately, William set about trying to win freedom for the imprisoned Friends. He traveled to Dublin, where he petitioned the lord lieutenant, the king's representative, to free the Quakers. He wrote letters to some high-ranking officials and spoke with others. He tried again and again to win freedom for the suffering Friends.

For the next several months, he split his time between taking care of business matters for the admiral and continuing his work on behalf of the Friends. One week, he and Philip Ford would collect rents and settle disputes between tenants. The next, he would visit high-ranking officials to plead on behalf of those in jail. Finally, in early June 1670, he convinced the lord lieutenant of Ireland to free all the Friends imprisoned in that land.

Not long before William won freedom for the persecuted Irish Friends, Sir William had written to him: "I wish you had . . . done all the business there and that you were here for I find myself to decline."[2] Though not yet fifty years of age, the admiral was ill and tired. He knew he was dying. He wanted his son to come home, to be by his side.

In late July or early August, with the Irish Quakers free from prison and his father's work finished, William set sail for England, leaving Ford in Ireland to oversee the Penn estates.

In the months that William had been gone, affairs had not gone well for the English Friends. Parliament was more fearful than ever that King Charles II—the son of a Catholic mother—would reestablish Catholicism in England. The Conventicle Act, originally passed in 1664 to punish religious nonconformists, was given new teeth in the spring of 1670, shortly before William arrived back in London. According to the act, any English man or woman over the age of sixteen who met at any assembly (or conventicle) to practice any religion other than the Church of England faced fines, the loss of all property, and imprisonment. Catholics could avoid persecution by practicing their faith in secret—and many did. Quakers, however, believed they had a moral obligation to test the act. Some, including George Fox, allowed themselves to be arrested, hoping their arrests would cause the government to reconsider its persecution of the Quakers. Not long after William's return, he announced that he and a fellow Quaker, William Mead, would hold a religious service at a meetinghouse on Christchurch Street, not far from the house in which William was born.

On August 14, when Mead and William showed up at the meetinghouse, they found the doorway blocked by constables. The street outside was packed with people, including many who were there in hope of seeing trouble break out between the Quakers and the authorities. William began to address the crowd. Immediately, he and Mead were arrested. Unfortunately, as the two Quakers were being led away, a scuffle broke out in the crowd.

At first, Penn and Mead were held in the Black Dog Tavern, near Newgate Prison on the west side of London. The Black Dog was what was known as a "sponging house" of the prison. Its bailiff, or jailer, "sponged" on prisoners who were awaiting trial, growing rich by charging them outrageous prices for food and drink and a cramped space to sleep. While the authorities wanted to make an example of the admiral's son, they were probably afraid to place a known friend of the king and duke of York in the hellhole known as Newgate before he was convicted of a crime.

Soon after his arrest, William wrote to his father. From the tone of the letter, we know the reconciliation between father and son was almost complete. "My Dear Father . . . ," he wrote, " . . . be not displeased nor grieved. . . . I doubt not but I may be at liberty in a day or two, to see thee. I am very well, and have no trouble upon my spirits, besides my absence from thee. . . . What they have to charge me with is harmless. . . ."[3]

William's idea that he would be released in a day or two proved wrong. It took two weeks before he and Mead were taken from the Black Dog to the Old Bailey. The first order of business was a reading of the charges against the two men. As the recorder rose in the stone-walled courtroom and read the charges, William discovered that he and Mead were not charged with a "harmless" violation of the Conventicle Act. Instead, because of the scuffle, they were charged with disturbing the peace. According to the indictment, Penn and Mead, with about three hundred other persons, had gathered together "with force and arms . . . against the peace of the . . . King, his Crown and dignity."[4] Instead of a hearing before a magistrate, they would be tried by a jury of twelve men. If they were found guilty of this more serious charge they would be considered traitors, and as traitors they could be put to death.

The actual trial did not start for two more days. On September 3, Penn and Mead were led into the courtroom once again. As they entered, a bailiff snatched their hats from their heads. The chief judge, Sir Samuel Starling, ordered that their hats be replaced. As soon as the bailiff clapped their hats back on, Sir Samuel fined each of the Quakers for wearing their hats in court.

Penn immediately showed he had a sense of humor, even when faced with injustice. "I desire it might be observed that we came into the court with our hats taken off," he said, "and if they have been put on since, it was by order from the [judge]; and therefore not we, but the [judge] should be fined."[5]

Soon, his sense of humor would be tested. So would his sense of justice, for the trial was a mockery. Sir Samuel showed his prejudice again and again. He insulted William's father. He called only prosecution witnesses and would not allow William, who was acting as his own lawyer and as Mead's, to question them. Still, William was able to argue that as an Englishman he had the right to pray and worship as he saw fit. He also argued that the trial was a travesty that threatened the rights of every Englishman. Sir Samuel lost his temper. He ordered the bailiffs to lock William in the baildock, a portable cell like a big birdcage. As he was led away, William angrily shouted to the crowd in the courtroom. "Is this justice or true judgment? Must I . . . be taken away because I plead for the fundamental laws of England?"[6]

Mead was no more willing to be railroaded than Penn. Soon, he too was locked in the bail-dock. By the time the jury was ready to consider its verdict, its members—who must have known that Quakers would never gather "with force and arms" to disturb the peace—had been completely alienated by the judge's behavior. After a brief deliberation, jury foreman Edward Bushel announced that it had found Mead innocent and Penn guilty only of speaking in the street. Of course, speaking in the street was not a crime, not even under the Conventicle Act.

Furious, the judge tried to convince the jurors to change their verdict. Still, Bushel and the others on the jury stood by their original finding. Sir Samuel should have accepted the jury's findings. Instead, he ordered the jury members locked up. "Gentlemen," the court recorder said, "you shall not be dismissed till we have a verdict that the court will accept, and you shall be locked up without meat, drink, fire, and tobacco. We will have a verdict, by the help of God, or you shall starve for it."[7]

Still, the jurors refused to budge. Finally, after two nights in cold, bare cells without food or water, Bushel announced that the jury had, indeed, changed its verdict. Now, the jury foreman said, both Penn and Mead were found not guilty of all charges. Sir Samuel had to accept the verdict. Furious, however, he fined each juror for contempt. Since neither they nor the two Quakers could pay their fines, all were sent to Newgate Prison.

Newgate was not like the Tower of London where the highborn were held; it was the prison that housed common criminals. It was crowded and filthy, filled with disease and depravity. William, though, found the worst part of his imprisonment being away from his father who, by that time, was near death. "I am more concerned at thy [illness] and the pains that attend it, than at my own mere imprisonment . . . ," he wrote on September 5.[8]

The admiral wanted to see his son again before he died. He must have offered to pay William's fine. William quickly wrote asking his father not to pay. "I intreat thee," he said, "not to purchase my liberty."[9]

The admiral knew he did not have time to wait for William to win his freedom by legal means. Without telling his son, he sent a messenger to the prison with money to free both him and Mead. Eight of the jurors also bought their freedom, though Bushel and three others remained in Newgate for two months until the appeal of their fines reached a higher court. Later, the Lord Chief Justice of England ruled that Sir Samuel was wrong in his treatment of the jurors. Thanks to the courage of Penn, Mead, and the jurors, an important legal precedent was set guaranteeing that English juries (and later juries in America) would be free from tampering by judges.

As soon as William gained his freedom, he rushed to the Penn house in Wanstead. There he found his father near death. For the next ten days, William hardly left the admiral's side. At some time during this period, the elder Penn sent a message to the duke of York and to the king asking his old friends to protect his son in the years ahead, for he knew that William's Quakerism could result in the loss of his lands, his fortune, even his life. Soon, the admiral got the assurances he needed.

With that done, the admiral, just forty-nine years old, prepared for his death. "Son William," he said, "I am weary of the world; I would not live my days over again, if I could command them at a wish; for the snares of life are greater than the fears of death."[10]

In those days, as he reflected on his life, the admiral came to feel some sympathy for William's beliefs. William later wrote: "Wearied to live, as well as near to die, he took his leave of us, and of me, with this expression, and a most composed countenance: 'Son William . . . , keep to your plain way of preaching, and keep to your plain way of living. . . .' " Then, William added, his father spoke his last words. "Bury me by my mother. Live all in love. Shun all manner of evil. And I pray God to bless you all, and He will bless you."[11]

The admiral died on September 16, 1670. William Penn the younger now had to stand as a man in his own right.

EIGHT

"A Match of Providence's Making"

William Penn arranged a hero's funeral for his father. Three companies of foot soldiers led a solemn procession through the streets of Bristol, the city of Sir William's birth. The flags of the fleets he had commanded flew over the marchers' heads, along with the red pennant of a General-of-the-Sea. At the head of the procession, soldiers carried the suit of armor he had worn on the deck of the *Royal Charles* during sea battles with the Dutch. At the rear of the procession, followed by the mourners, the admiral's coffin was borne on a hearse drawn by six matched horses.

Sir William was, as he had wished, buried next to his mother in the steeplehouse of St. Mary Redclyffe. His armor was placed next to his tomb, as if standing guard over the body of the man many still consider one of England's greatest naval heroes. His battle flags were hung on a wall nearby, surrounding a bronze plaque erected soon after the funeral. On that plaque a lengthy commemorative message written by his son described his father's life and accomplishments.

As the admiral's firstborn son, William was left virtually his entire estate. He inherited Irish and English estates with thousands of acres and rents that amounted to about fifteen hundred pounds a year, a small fortune at a time when many professional men earned twenty pounds per year or less. In addition, he was given the gold medal and chain his father had been awarded by Oliver Cromwell following the defeat of the Dutch in 1653.

The admiral's other survivors were also provided for. Lady Margaret, William's mother, was left the use of the house in Wanstead for the balance of her life, a comfortable income, and most of his jewels. Richard, William's brother, was bequeathed the admiral's guns and swords, along with a diamond ring and several hundred pounds. Peg, already married to a wealthy man, was given a small amount of money.

For a time, Penn lived with his mother and brother at the Wanstead manor house. Soon, though, he found lodgings in a village about five miles from Amersham, where Guli lived with her mother and stepfather. After the death of his father and all the legal troubles he had faced in London, time in the country, near the woman he loved, must have been a healing tonic for his heart and soul.

Because of Penn's traveling and his arrests and time in prison, he and Guli had spent little time together since they agreed to marry two years earlier. Now they were able to walk and talk together and attend meetings with other Friends who lived in and around Amersham.

William and Guli must have been a striking couple. Guli was, as noted earlier, a beautiful young woman.

An engraving of her, copied from a painting made by an unknown artist some time after her marriage to William, shows a woman with fine, sensitive features. Always sickly, she appears somewhat preoccupied, as if she is thinking about an uncertain future. Her clothing, while plain compared with the dresses worn at the Court, was fancy compared with the muted dresses worn by many Quaker women. Penn, like Guli, favored fancy clothes, even after his conversion. In fact, while wearing simple clothes was encouraged by the Friends, it was not a requirement of the Quaker faith. Penn himself never gave up his love for the styles of the Cavaliers, though he did wear the plain coats and breeches favored by the Quakers when preaching. But even then he wore silver buckles on his shoes and, often, a vest or sash of sky-blue silk. He also continued wearing a wig, as he had through much of his life. Later in his life, Penn's wig caused a few Quakers to question his sincerity. At least one went so far as to accuse him of pride. At that time, George Fox came to his defense.

Penn, he said in a letter to a Friend, lost his hair "when but 3 years ould . . . by ye small Pox . . . [and] when kept a close Prisoner in ye Tower . . . his hair shed away: and since [then] he has worn a very short civil thing." Penn, he added, wore his wig "to keep his head & ears warm & not for pride." Then Fox, who was never afraid to admonish his followers, said the Quaker who had complained of Penn's wig, a woman named Sarah Harris, should look to her own salvation and not worry so much about William Penn's.[1]

Thanks to his inheritance, Penn was free to dedicate his life to the Quaker cause. He soon began trav-

eling to meetings around Amersham. He visited Oxford, where he investigated the troubles of Friends who
were being punished under the Conventicle Act. He
wrote letters on behalf of imprisoned Quakers. During
these months the authorities, particularly Sir Samuel
Starling, who was still smarting over his legal defeat,
were keeping a careful watch on him, waiting for him
to make another mistake. Soon, he did.

In London, on February 5, 1671, Penn was at a
meeting when, suddenly, soldiers came and planted
themselves in the meetinghouse doorway. He could
have avoided trouble if he had simply sat still. Instead,
he once again chose to challenge the law. He stood,
walked to the front of the room, and began preaching.
The soldiers allowed him to speak for a time, then they
ran forward, grabbed him, and pulled him from the
room. Once again, William found himself being led to
the Tower of London.

A trial was held that night. The judges included Sir
John Robinson, the lieutenant of the tower, who had
been Penn's jailer during his first imprisonment, and
Starling. Penn was charged with breaking a law known
as the Oxford Five Mile Act. This act made it a crime
for any nonconforming clergyman to come within five
miles of any town or city where they had preached at
an unlawful meeting.

Quickly, Penn told the court that he had never been
a clergyman. "That of all laws can't concern me," he
said.[2] He went on to successfully argue that he could
not be prosecuted or punished under the law. Sir Samuel
and the others on the court, however, wanted to make
an example of him. They asked him to swear an oath
that he would not take up arms against the king.

Why, Penn asked, would they require him to swear not to take up arms when, as a Quaker, he was nonviolent? "Should I swear not to do what is already against my conscience to do?" he asked.[3]

Though the judges could have ordered him taken away as soon as he refused to swear an oath, they attacked him personally.

"I vow, Mr. Penn, I am sorry for you. . .," Sir John said. "Why should you render yourself unhappy by associating with such simple people [as the Quakers]?"

Because, William answered, "I have made it my choice to relinquish the company of those that are . . . wicked."

"You have been as bad as other men," Sir John quickly retorted.

At that, William grew angry. "When and where?" he asked. "I charge you to tell the company to my face. . . . I make this bold challenge to all men, women, and children upon the earth, justly to accuse me of ever having seen me drunk, heard me swear, utter a curse, or speak one obscene word. . . . I trample thy slander as dirt under my feet."

"Well," Sir John said, "I must send you to Newgate for six months. . . ."[4]

And so Penn was led again to Newgate. Though his wealth could have purchased him some comforts in the prison, he was housed with common criminals. He and other prisoners were allowed a few hours of exercise each day, but most of the time they were locked in a large, round room. At the center of that room there was a great pillar that supported the floor of a chapel above. At night, prisoners tied three tiers of hammocks to that pillar, for sleeping. The sick and dying lay on pallets on the floor. At about the time Penn was imprisoned, a jury investigating the death of a prisoner came to Newgate and looked in the door of the round room where Penn was held. "Lord Bless me," cried the jury foreman, "what a sight is here? I did not think there had been so much cruelty in the hearts of Englishmen." Instead of wondering how a prisoner died in Newgate, he went on, the jury should instead wonder how any of the men in the prison managed to stay alive.[5]

William put his six months in prison to good use. Somehow, in that crowded, disease-infested place, where it was not unusual for the skulls of executed men and women to be used as playthings by hardened criminals, he managed to write several more Quaker pamphlets and letters protesting the treatment of Friends in and out of prison. Through his writing at this time, the central theme was that all people have a God-given right to follow their consciences in matters of religion. He also wrote an answer to a pamphlet written by Sir Samuel Starling attacking Penn, Mead, and William's late father. In his response, a pamphlet titled *Truth Rescued from Impostors*, he not only defended freedom of belief but also the fundamental legal rights of Englishmen, and his father's reputation as a naval hero.

Finally, in late July or early August 1671, Penn was released from the "common stinking jail," as he called Newgate.[6] Immediately, he traveled to be with Guli. While they were happy together, they had little time to enjoy each other's company. In mid-August, he once again said good-bye to her and departed on a missionary journey. For the next two months he and two other Quakers journeyed through the Netherlands and Germany, where they met with leaders of nonconformist religious groups, exchanging views and trying to win converts.

On October 24, 1671, William returned to England, landing in Harwich, not far from London. As a Quaker leader, his comings and goings were noticed by informers who reported to the English government. "On Tuesday out of one of our packet boats from Holland arrived here Sir William Penn's eldest son, the great opinionist. He went presently and associated himself with the Quakers of this town," one such informer noted soon after Penn's return from the Continent.[7]

At that time, George Fox was in America, visiting small, scattered Quaker communities that had been established along the eastern seaboard. With Fox absent, Penn assumed a position of leadership in the Quaker movement. But not everything in his life was Quaker business. Early in 1672, he returned to London and, from there, traveled to Amersham to be with Guli. On February 7, he and his bride-to-be appeared before the Friends at a meeting in the home of a local Friend and announced their plans to marry.

In accordance with the Quaker way, the question of whether William and Guli should marry was referred to two members of the meeting. To no one's surprise, the two members, one of whom was Thomas Ellwood, Guli's longtime friend, found no reason why the two should not marry.

At about the same time that Guli and Penn announced their plans to marry, Quakers and other religious nonconformists in England were told they no longer had to fear official reprisals because of their religious beliefs. At that time, King Charles was involved

in secret negotiations with the king of France. He
wanted that country's help in a looming war with Holland. To get help from the Catholic king and to end
dissension at home, Charles issued what was known as
the Declaration of Indulgence. This declaration suspended all laws that punished Catholics, Quakers, and
other nonconformists because of religious beliefs or
practices.

On April 4, 1672, with this news making the occasion even more joyous, Penn and Guli were married.
The ceremony took place in the low-ceilinged, stone-
walled great hall at King's Farm, a fourteenth-century
structure in Amersham that was once used as a royal
hunting lodge. Only a few friends were in attendance
as William and Guli sat side by side, in silence, gathering their thoughts. When both were ready, they held
hands and stood. In simple words, without fanfare, they
declared their love and pledged their lives to each other.
Then they sat again in silent meditation and prayer. As
was the Quaker custom, there was no preacher, there
were no rings, no organ music, and no promises of
obedience.

Following the ceremony, the wedding guests, including William's mother and brother, gathered at a
nearby house. Ellwood, who served as clerk of the
meeting, drew up a formal marriage certificate and
passed it around so all could sign as witnesses. Soon,
Guli and William left the party, riding to the village of
Rickmansworth in a new coach he had specially built
for the occasion. There they began their married life in
Basing House, a rented home surrounded by a walled
garden and towering linden trees.

From the beginning of their married life, William and Guli were happy with each other. His marriage, he later said, "was a match of Providence's making" to a woman who was "the joy of my life." And Guli loved him every bit as much as he loved her. She was, in his words, his "love and delight," loving him "with a deep and upright love."[8]

They would need all their love for each other in the years ahead. For William Penn the times of trial were not yet over, and times of great sorrow were about to begin.

NINE

Years of Trial,
Years of Change

Following his marriage to Guli, William Penn enjoyed a brief period of peace and contentment. "I am at peace with all men," he wrote at that time.[1] And he had reasons to be happy. Basing House was a spacious, comfortable manor in the beautiful Thames Valley, west of London. Guli's family lived nearby, as did a large circle of Quakers, so the Penns were surrounded by caring Friends. At the same time, the Declaration of Indulgence issued by Charles II meant he could go to meetings and write without fear of arrest. For Penn, the first months of his honeymoon were a welcome vacation.

By the time the couple moved into Basing House, Philip Ford, the Quaker who Penn had left in charge of the Irish estate, had finished his work at Shanagarry and returned to England where Penn gave him virtually full control of his money. He even allowed Ford to carry his change purse to pay everyday expenses.

In fact, despite his wealth, which had grown greater with his marriage to Guli, Penn had no head for business. He was careless and often let bills go unpaid. He trusted Ford so much that he typically signed legal documents and bills Ford presented for payment without even bothering to read them. Ford's help made it possible for Penn to devote even more time to his writing and to missionary journeys in the south of England.

Only a few months after William's marriage, Parliament rescinded the Declaration of Indulgence and passed a law that required English men and women to swear an oath of allegiance to the Crown. While the act was aimed at Catholics in government service, it was widely used to once again fill England's jails and prisons with Quakers who refused to swear the oath.

At about this time, Fox returned to England from America. As the founder of the Quakers, he was a marked man. In December 1673, after speaking to a meeting held in a barn in Worcestershire, Fox was sitting with a few Friends in the parlor of a nearby house when a justice of the peace broke in and arrested him. He was charged with holding religious meetings "upon a pretence of exercise of religion otherwise than what is established by the law of England."[2]

At his trial, held several months after his arrest, the justices soon realized that the case against Fox was weak because he had not even been at a meeting when he was arrested. Still, they wanted the troublesome Quaker off the street. And they knew they had a way to achieve that goal.

"You, Mr. Fox . . . will you take the Oath of Allegiance and Supremacy?" asked one of the justices. Of course Fox answered that he would not—and could not—as a Quaker. "I never took an oath in my life," he answered, "but I [have] always been true to the Government."[3]

Fox was thrown back into jail. Now, though, he was charged under an ancient English law as an enemy of the Crown. It was immediately obvious to Penn and other Quakers that if something wasn't done to gain Fox's freedom, he might die behind bars. For the next fourteen months, Penn fought to gain Fox's freedom. He wrote letters and appeared in court. He still had some influence with government leaders and he used that influence. Sometime in the following year, he gained an audience with James, the duke of York. The duke received Penn and William Mead (the same Mead who had stood trial with William several years earlier) warmly. James, Penn later said, "told us that he was against all persecution for the sake of religion. . . ."[4] The conversation, Penn said, then became more personal. "[The duke] was pleased to take very particular notice of me," he said, "both for the relation my father had had to his service in the navy, and the care he promised to show in my regard. . . ."[5]

James apparently spoke to his brother Charles II about the Fox case, for Penn soon wrote to Fox, reporting that "a great lord, a man of noble mind" was intervening with the king to obtain his release.[6] Finally, in early 1675, after more than a year behind bars, Fox was set free.

During this same period, as Penn worked to gain the Quaker leader's freedom, he also became directly involved in the Quaker settlement of America for the first time. As the result of a complicated legal battle, he was named one of three trustees to administer a tract of land owned by the Friends in what was then known as West New Jersey. As a trustee, Penn helped organize the settlement of the territory. He also helped write a charter of government called "Concessions and Agreements." The most liberal and enlightened document of its kind then in existence, it included many of the provisions that he later would make part of the charter for the Pennsylvania colony. It affirmed all the basic rights and privileges enjoyed by citizens of England but also included complete freedom of religion and gave the people the power to make laws.

During the time of Fox's imprisonment, the burden that Penn carried for the Quaker movement was almost overwhelming. In addition to his legal work on behalf of the founder, and in connection with the settlement of West New Jersey, he had to answer frequent attacks against the Friends by Protestant churchmen. He answered these attacks in print and in public debates with non Quaker ministers.

These public debates were popular events in seventeenth century England. Men, women, and children attended in droves, much the way they attend sporting events today. At one such debate that pitted Penn and several other Quakers against a group of Baptist ministers, more than six thousand people showed up to listen and cheer or jeer. After that debate, Penn wrote to Fox that "all coffee houses and such like public places are filled with news of it. . . ."[7]

During these years, as Penn labored on behalf of Fox and the Quakers, he and Guli suffered one heartbreaking personal loss after another.

Childbirth in the seventeenth century was risky. About one in four infants died before reaching the age of ten; and many women died giving birth or soon after due to infections. Frail ever since a bout of smallpox suffered as a young adult, Guli was particularly at risk. Soon after her marriage to William, she became pregnant and, on January 23, 1673, she gave birth to a baby girl, Gulielma Maria. The baby lived only about seven weeks. She was buried in the graveyard by the Jordans Meeting House, not far from where the Penns lived.

The baby's death was followed almost immediately by the death of eighteen-year-old Richard Penn, William's brother, probably of smallpox. While Penn's thoughts and feelings at this time are not known, it is easy to imagine him struggling to understand how and why his baby girl and then his brother, Dickie, were taken. As a good Quaker, though, he would have found solace in his faith.

Still, though, the dying was not over. On February 28, 1674, Guli gave birth to twins, a boy named William and a girl, Mary. Like the baby the Penns had buried just a year earlier, these infants were small and frail. William, the baby boy, died just a few weeks after his birth. Mary clung to life.

For a time, Penn curtailed his traveling as much as possible so he could stay close to Guli and his surviving baby daughter. During these difficult months, as the baby grew weaker, Guli became pregnant once again. In January 1675, she gave birth to a fourth child, a healthy, strong boy that the Penns named Springett, after Guli's father. The joy of the boy's birth, however, was tainted just a few weeks later when Mary, the girl born about a year earlier, died.

With all the tragedies in his life, it would have been understandable if Penn had stopped working for the Quaker cause. Instead, he worked harder, probably because he found relief from his personal anguish in his work. In any case, the Quakers needed him. Though Fox was freed from prison at about the same time Springett Penn was born, the persecution of the Friends and other religious nonconformists continued. In the months following Fox's release, Penn wrote two tracts. In the first of these, he argued that England could only be a great nation by granting religious and political freedom to all its citizens. In the second tract, *The Continued Cry of the Oppressed for Justice*, he listed—simply and without comment—the sufferings of Quakers in England, county by county. He wrote of Friends in prison, fined, treated brutally by the authorities, their property taken or destroyed, in the hope that the list would somehow appeal to the humanity of the king and the members of Parliament.

At about this time, Penn moved his family to a new house near the village of Worminghurst, in Sussex. The two-story, red-brick manor house, part of a large inheritance that Guli had been left by her father, sat high on a hill surrounded by dense woods. On a clear day, the waters of the English Channel could be seen glittering in the distance about six miles away. Best of all, the house was washed over by refreshing sea breezes. The Penns hoped the new location would be healthier than Basing House, where they had lost three children.

It was probably at Worminghurst that Penn truly fell in love with country living. Life at Worminghurst was well ordered and quiet. The family rose at five on summer mornings, seven in winter, and at six in other months. After morning worship and breakfast, the family and servants took care of chores. At eleven, all gathered to read the Bible and, at noon, to eat dinner. Work filled the afternoon hours, followed by another religious meeting at six. That meeting was followed by supper, at which time all reported on their day's activities. All were in bed soon after sunset.

Indeed, in accord with the Quaker belief that the outward life must be a reflection of inward beliefs, all activities at the house centered on the Quaker faith. Meetings, with as many as two hundred Friends in attendance, were regularly held in the manor's huge drawing room. And in his study there Penn wrote tirelessly, defending and explaining the Quaker way of life and beliefs.

In July 1677, he and several other Friends, including George Fox, departed on another missionary trip to Holland and Germany. As on his first missionary journey, audiences listened politely, but few joined the Society of Friends. In Germany, however, he established contacts that would later result in the emigration of a large number of German colonists to Pennsylvania.

Returning to England in late 1677, Penn spent most of the next year toiling to ease the persecution of Quakers who were being punished for their faith. In November, he visited Worminghurst but only stayed a short time. In a letter to Margaret Fox, he said that Springett, then three years old, had grown to be "a large and active child." Guli, who was expecting another child, was "all well."[8] That child, born on March 6, 1678, was a healthy baby girl. Named Letitia, but called Tish by her father, she was destined to live a long and healthy life.

Not long after the baby's birth, Penn went before the House of Commons (one of the two houses of Parliament) to argue in favor of religious tolerance. Specifically, he wanted the lawmakers to change a law that required all English men and women to swear an oath of allegience to the king. He wanted the law rewritten so that Quakers could "affirm" their allegiance without taking an oath. The problem, he told the lawmakers, was not that Quakers were disloyal; it was that Quakers obeyed Jesus' command not to swear oaths.

The Quakers, he said, "have been as the . . . common whipping stock of the kingdom; all laws have been let loose upon us, as if the design were not to reform, but to destroy us; and this, not for what we are, but for what we are not. . . ."

Penn also spoke up on behalf of Catholics.

"I am far from thinking it fit, because I exclaim against the injustice of whipping Quakers, that Papists should be whipped for their consciences," he said "No . . . we must give the liberty we ask. . . . for we . . . would have none suffer for a truly sober and conscientious dissent. . . ."[9]

Penn's speeches ultimately convinced the lawmakers to grant his request. Unfortunately, an Anglican minister named Titus Oates chose that time to begin circulating wild rumors of what he called the "Popish Plot." Catholics, Oates said, were plotting to murder Charles II so that the duke of York, a Catholic, could be crowned king. These rumors threw the country into turmoil, forcing Charles II to disband Parliament before the Quakers received the legal relief that Penn had asked for.

By this time, Penn was beginning to despair that he and the other Friends would ever gain the freedom they wanted by pleading with the king. During the next two years, he continued striving in the Quaker cause, but he also turned his attention to the world of politics. In

1679 he backed his old friend Algernon Sidney in his bid to be elected to Parliament. Sidney, whom William first met in France in 1665 and whose ideas about tolerance and the rights of man had helped shaped Penn's own beliefs, had been allowed back into England in 1677, ending his long period of exile. Now he wanted to bring his liberal ideas to government, hoping that he and like-minded men might be elected to Parliament and then be in a position to persuade the king to grant more political and religious freedom to the people of England.

While Penn was a friend of both the king and the duke of York, he supported Sidney, a non-Royalist, because he believed in his heart it was the right thing to do. Twice Sidney was elected to Parliament, and twice rival politicians used trickery to keep him from the seat he had won. Disheartened, Sidney refused to try again. He was sick of the whole process.

By that time, Penn, too, was discouraged. He had tried every way he knew to gain freedom of conscience for the Friends in England. His speeches, his writings, his personal example had all been in vain. With his wealth and Guli's he could easily have retired to a life of ease at Worminghurst or in Ireland. His fame, and the protection of the king and duke of York, would have guaranteed his safety. But Penn was not suited to a life of inaction. Instead, he turned his attention across the sea, to America. William Penn was about to begin the greatest adventure of his life.

TEN

The Seed of a Nation

"There is no hope in England," William Penn said in the spring of 1680. Preaching the idea of freedom of conscience to the English was, he added, like trying to play music to charm "a deaf adder."[1]

Convinced, finally, that England would never give the Quakers the freedom they desired, he resolved to found his own colony in America. Surely there, far from England with its religious intolerance, the Quakers would be free to practice their faith without fear of imprisonment or worse.

The Quakers could have emigrated to the West New Jersey colony where a few Friends were already living in peace. But Penn had a greater vision. He envisioned thousands of Friends and other dissenting Christians fleeing persecution in England, Ireland, Scotland, Holland, and Germany. These thousands would need more land than was available in Jersey. Also, Jersey already had a government in place, a society established. Penn wanted to establish something completely, a God-centered society based on ideas that had been simmering in his mind, like a pot of stew left slowly cooking over an open flame, ever since his Oxford days.

Penn knew that to the west and north of the Jersey colony there was a vast amount of virgin land just waiting to be settled. He also knew he couldn't simply ask Charles II for land in America. While the king might have been receptive to the idea because of his long friendship with William's father, his followers and advisors would have been outraged. Penn had to present Charles with some logical excuse for giving him the land he wanted.

He found the excuse he needed when he recalled that the Crown owed his father a large sum of money for loans the admiral had made to the king during the Dutch wars. This money—about sixteen thousand pounds—was now owed to Penn as his father's heir. On June 1, 1680, Penn petitioned the Crown for a grant of land between Maryland and New York. In exchange for that land, he promised to forgive the debt.

For nine months, the petition made its way from one government office to another. Finally Penn was given the legal document known as a charter granting him ownership of a huge tract of land running westward from the Delaware River north from Maryland to New York. Perhaps to avoid claims by others to whom the Crown owed money, no mention was made in the charter of the debt owed to William's father. Instead, the charter said the king gave Penn the land "in the memorie . . . of his late father. . . ."[2]

There was, no doubt, another reason why the king approved Penn's petition. By giving the Friends land in America, he guaranteed that shiploads of dissident Quakers and other nonconformists would soon be gone from England. Penn himself believed this was the real reason why the charter was granted. In a letter written to a friend years later, he said, "The government at home was glad to be rid of us at so cheap a rate."[3]

The charter was signed by the king on March 4, 1681. According to a famous story, when Penn entered the chamber where Charles was to sign the document, he did not remove his hat, as courtesy and protocol demanded. The king, who was expected to keep his head covered at all times, responded by removing his own feather-bedecked hat. At that, William said, "Friend Charles, why dost thou uncover?" Charles, so the story goes, answered, "Because it is the custom here for only one man to wear a hat."[4]

Penn's charter made him the sole proprietor of the largest territory ever owned by a private citizen. He owned the land, all the living things in its forests and waters, and all the precious metals and gems that might be discovered there. He could make laws with the approval of the province's freemen and do whatever else was necessary for the establishment of justice, provided he did not break the laws of England. He could sell or rent lands and establish towns and counties. In exchange for these privileges, he had to pay the Crown "two Beaver Skins to bee delivered att our . . . Castle of Windsor, on the first day of January, in every yeare; and also the fifth parte of all Gold and silver Oare."[5]

The king had one other requirement. He wanted the colony to be named in honor of Sir William. It was to be called Pennsylvania, Latin for "Penn's Woods." Penn tried in vain to convince the monarch to let him name the colony "Sylvania" or "New Wales," but Charles knew what he wanted. When Penn said he was afraid people would think he had named the colony for himself because of vanity, the king still refused to change the name.

Penn immediately began promoting his new province. He published two tracts describing the area's native inhabitants, climate, soil, vegetation, wildlife, and geography. He also sent letters to his contacts in Germany, Holland, and France telling them of his grant. He offered land for sale and established fees for passage to America.

In mid-April, Penn sent his cousin William Markham to Pennsylvania to serve as provisional governor until he could make the journey. Markham was instructed to find a site for a great city Penn dreamed of and a location for Penn's residence. He was also told to establish good relations with the Native Americans in the province and the two thousand or so European colonists who lived along the Delaware River and who were now Penn's subjects. Markham took with him a letter from Penn promising these settlers they had nothing to fear from him as their Proprietor. ". . .you are now fixt, at the mercy of no Governor that comes to make his fortune great," he said, "you shall be governed by laws of your own making, and live a free . . . people. I shall not usurp the right of any, or oppress his person. . . . In short, whatever . . . free men can reasonably desire for the security and improvement of their own happiness, I shall heartily comply with. . . ."[6]

Another letter written at about the same time explained that Penn's purpose in founding Pennsylvania was to establish "a holy experiment" that would serve as "an example . . . to the nations."[7] It was to be an experiment unlike any ever tried before: an experiment to prove that people could govern themselves and live in peace and love by following the will of God and by respecting the rights of others.

Meanwhile, the parcels of land Penn offered for sale—five thousand acres for one hundred pounds and an annual rent of one shilling per one hundred acres—were quickly snapped up by buyers. By July, just three months after King Charles signed the Pennsylvania Charter, shiploads of Quakers and other nonconformists were heading across the Atlantic to the new colony.

At that time, Penn met with a group of settlers who had purchased land and not yet departed. Together, they drew up a provisional plan for the government of Pennsylvania. During much of the next year, Penn sought advice and counsel from some of the foremost political thinkers in Europe, including his old friend Algernon Sidney, as he revised and rewrote the plan more than a dozen times. Finally, in July 1682, Penn's "First Frame of Government" was ready.

According to the First Frame, the province's government would be headed by a governor—initially Penn himself or someone he appointed—with limited powers. This governor would work with an elected council of seventy-two members and an elected general assembly of as many as five hundred members. Together, the governor, the council, and the assembly would make laws and perform the other business of the province, though Penn, as governor, would have the power to veto proposed legislation.

The document included ideas that anticipated the Declaration of Independence. While public officeholders had to be Christians, any person who believed in God was welcome to live in the colony. No persons were to be "molested or prejudiced for their religious persuasion, or practice, in matters of faith and worship," nor would they be "compelled, at any time, to frequent or maintain any religious worship, place or ministry whatsoever."[8]

In addition, the First Frame guaranteed free elections and gave the right to vote to all "freeholders" (men who owned property). It stipulated that no taxes could be levied without the approval of the voters. It guaranteed jury trials without interference by government officials or judges. Remembering his own time in the Tower of London and Newgate, Penn paid particular attention to the rights of prisoners. The Frame of Government also stipulated that all children over the age of twelve were to be taught a trade or skill, and it protected the rights of the colony's Native Americans, guaranteeing that any Indian charged with a crime would be tried by a jury made up of six settlers and six Indians.

Some critics, including Sidney, complained that the Frame of Government did not ban slavery or the slave trade. A similar document that Penn had written for the province of West New Jersey contained the provision that "all and every person . . . shall . . . be free from oppression and slavery."[9]

Penn did argue several issues with the assembly in an attempt to curtail slavery in his province: that slaves should be freed after fourteen years of servitude, that their marriages should be recognized, and that slave families should not be broken up through indiscriminate selling of family members. Even these steps, however, were stopped as the assembly was, for the most part, composed of wealthy settlers who benefited by owning slaves.

That Penn would have done more on behalf of the slaves if he had been a perfect man can't be argued. Like all men, though, he wasn't perfect. In fact, he owned slaves himself, though he did make arrangements in his will that they were to be freed after his death. Perhaps he was frightened that if he moved too fast to ban slavery in Pennsylvania he would anger the king or authorities in England where slavery was a profitable business. In later years, the Pennsylvania Assembly did pass an act prohibiting the importation of slaves, but the act was quickly disallowed by the Crown. Slavery remained an institution in Pennsylvania until 1748, when the Quakers finally made it the first wholly free colony in America.

Even with this major drawback, the First Frame of Government was a remarkable document for its time. It gave sweeping freedoms to the inhabitants of Pennsylvania and guaranteed that no one man—not even its proprietor—would ever be able to control the lives of its residents.

Years later, Thomas Jefferson, speaking of Penn and this document, called him "the greatest lawgiver the world has produced; the first, either in ancient or modern times, who has laid the foundation of government in the pure and unadulterated principles of peace, of reason and right."[10]

As Penn worked on the Frame of Government, he began establishing friendly relations with the Indians living in Pennsylvania. In October 1761, he sent a letter to the Indian leaders. This letter read, in part:

> My Friends, . . . God hath been pleased to make me concerned in your parts of the world, and the king of the country where I live, hath given unto me a great province; but I desire to enjoy it with your love and consent. . . . I am very sensible of the unkindness and injustice that hath

been too much exercised toward you. . . . I am
not such a man. . . . I have great love and regard
towards you, and I desire to win and gain your
love and friendship, by a kind, just and peaceable life.

I shall shortly come to you myself. At which
time we may more . . . freely confer and [talk]
of these matters.

"I am your loving friend, William Penn."[11]

In the months following the granting of the charter, Penn
also began planning a great city with broad, tree-lined
streets, laid out in a grid, without the crowding and clut-
ter of London. He planned a city with houses surrounded
by lawns and gardens, with parks and open areas. He
wanted a city, he said, like "a green country town, which
will never be burned, and always be wholesome."[12]

While Penn was working to build the foundations
for his colony and preparing for his own departure, he
took time to write a new version of No Cross, No
Crown, the Quaker tract written in prison a dozen years
earlier. This new version was not simply a revision of
his older work, it was a completely new book that explained in detail the Quaker beliefs. Today, this book is
considered Penn's most important religious work.

In early 1682, Penn suffered a great loss when his
mother died. Though he had not seen Lady Margaret
very often after his conversion, the love they felt for
each other had never weakened. Her death hit William
hard. His grieving, though, could not last long. There
was too much work to do.

Finally, in August of that same year, he was ready
to depart for America with Guli and their three chil-

This wood engraving is a copy of an original oil painting by Howard Pyle, who liked to paint dramatic subjects such as this. The Quakers are looking back at their homeland as they set sail toward their future.

dren—Springett, aged seven; Tish, four; and the baby William Jr., born in early 1680. Very shortly before their departure, however, Guli fell ill. At the last minute, Penn had to sail to America alone to prepare a home for his family.

Before sailing for the New World, William wrote a long, farewell letter to Guli and his children. It was a letter filled with love. In it, he said he might never see them "more in this world." Indeed, ocean voyages in those days were dangerous, and many settlers died in the wilds of the American frontier.

"My dear wife!" he wrote to Guli, "remember thou wast the love of my youth, and much the joy of my life; the most beloved, as well as the most worthy of all my earthly comforts. . . ."[13]

He went on to write separate notes to each of his children, telling them to be good, to lead pious lives, to obey their mother in all things, and urging them to be honest and hardworking.

Penn left Worminghurst and traveled to the port of Deal where he joined about one hundred fellow Quakers on the *Welcome*. Moments before he climbed on board, Philip Ford showed up at dockside with several documents for him to sign. These documents included deeds conveying to Ford and his heirs three hundred thousand acres of land in the new colony unless Penn paid Ford three thousand pounds within two days. Ford, it seems, told Penn that the documents were simple accounts needing his signature for payment. Rushed, Penn scrawled his name on the papers without reading them. He then turned and walked up the gangplank to the ship that was to carry him to the land of Pennsylvania.

ELEVEN

The Holy Experiment

On August 31 or September 1, 1682, the *Welcome* set sail from the port city of Deal on England's southeast coast. The ship was a square-rigger, with three short, stubby masts that swayed from side to side as it wallowed in the North Atlantic swells. Only one hundred and eight feet in length, the *Welcome*'s hold was crammed with building materials, furniture, and settlers' belongings. Several horses, a few goats, and other work animals were housed in belowdecks stalls or tethered on deck. Barrels and crates and kegs filled with supplies were lashed wherever space allowed. All this cargo was destined to become part of the new settlement of Pennsylvania.

It took almost two months for the *Welcome* to cross the Atlantic. Most of the time, the Quakers huddled together in cramped, dank, almost airless quarters below deck. At night, they slept—when the tossing sea allowed sleep—on bare wooden bunks. Many were soon seasick, and the air below was heavy with the smells of vomit mixed with the stink of seldom-washed human bodies. During the voyage, smallpox broke out on the *Welcome* and spread quickly in the cramped and dirty quarters. Within days almost all the Friends were laid low.

Because Penn had had the disease as a boy, he was immune to infection, and was able to move freely among the sick, ministering to them without fear. He knelt by the suffering travelers and whispered words of encouragement and prayer. He bathed fevered brows with seawater. His presence and words of comfort filled the Quakers with hope and strength. A passenger, re-membering those days, later said that the care Penn gave the sick "was very advantageous to all the com-pany."[1] Still, by the time the disease ran its course, thirty-one Quakers had died.

On October 27, 1682, the *Welcome* came to an-chor in the Delaware River off the town of New Castle. Penn and the other passengers crowded the ship's rail looking almost hungrily at the small town and the thickly wooded land that lay all around. With darkness falling fast, though, they were forced to spend one more night on the cramped and smelly ship.

The next morning, the Quakers who had survived the voyage climbed over the ship's side and into boats to be rowed to shore. The entire town turned out to greet Penn and the other newcomers. Indians—Delawares and a few Iroquois—mingled with the settlers who lined the shore. The welcoming group included William Markham, the man Penn had sent to Pennsylvania im-mediately after receiving his grant; Thomas Holme, the colony's official surveyor; and officials of the English government. Quickly, Penn took possession of his prov-ince. In honor of the occasion, he was given a piece of turf with a twig stuck in it, along with a bowl of water and soil from the Delaware River, symbolizing his ownership of the lands, the forests, and the river.

From New Castle, the *Welcome* sailed up the Delaware. On October 29, at a village that had been named Upland by earlier Dutch settlers, Penn came ashore again. There he was greeted by a small contingent of Quakers who had made their way to America in the months since he got his charter, and by a number of Native Americans who wanted to see the "chief" who had written to them of peace and love. One of Penn's first official acts was to rename the settlement. Turning to one of the Friends who had been a fellow passenger on the *Welcome*, Penn said: "Providence has brought us here safe. Thou has been the companion of my perils. What wilt thou that I should call this place?" His companion, a man named Pearson, said, "Chester," in honor of his home city in England.[2]

While Penn is rightly honored as the founder of Pennsylvania, the colony was far from unsettled when he arrived. The lands he had been given by the king of England had, of course, been home to Native Americans for thousands of years before the first European settlers arrived. Most of these Indians—members of the Delaware, Shawnee, and Susquehana tribes, along with a few Iroquois—lived along the shores of the Delaware River. In addition, there were about two thousand Europeans, mostly Swedes and Dutch, living in the territories he was given. Now he was the ruler of those Europeans and all who would follow and of the Indians who lived on his lands.

Almost immediately, Penn left Chester and sailed in a small open boat up the Delaware. What he saw as the boat moved farther north must have filled him with awe. The river's surface was thick with wild ducks. Its banks teemed with wild cranes and plover. Impenetrable forests of black walnut, cedar, cypress, chestnut, hickory, beech, oak, walnut, and poplar trees stretched along both banks of the meandering river. Even from the boat, he was able to spy game in the forest: deer and elk, squirrels, rabbits, and wild turkey. This was a rich land, more than enough to welcome all the persecuted Christians in the world.

About four miles north of the place where the Schuylkill River joins the Delaware, Penn, Markham, and the others came to a spot the Indians called Coaquannock. This was the site that Holme had chosen for the construction of the great Quaker city Penn had envisioned. At that spot, the banks of the river rose high above the water. Below those bluffs, a small creek emptied into the Delaware, forming a natural harbor lined by a sandy shoreline. As Penn's boat turned toward shore, canoes raced from the beach to lead him and his party to land where a tiny village of ten houses stood in a clearing on the edge of the wilderness.

Penn had already decided on a name for his city. It was to be a place where all would live as brothers, in peace and love. What better name, then, than Philadelphia, taken from the Greek words *philos* and *adelphos*, meaning "love" and "brother."

From Philadelphia, Penn continued his journey, sailing about twenty-four miles farther north, to the spot Markham had chosen for the governor's estate. Markham, as Penn's agent, had already purchased a huge tract of land—almost six miles along one bank of the river—from the local Indians, paying for it with English currency, wampum, and merchandise. The

*Pennsbury, William Penn's home on the
Delaware river. It was destroyed by fire at the
end of the eighteenth century.*

house, to be called Pennsbury, may already have been
under construction by the time Penn inspected his estate. When completed, Pennsbury was a roomy, three-
story house of red brick with a tiled roof and wide
casement windows. Since the Delaware served as a
"highway" between the estate and Philadelphia, the
front of the house faced the river. A narrow, tree-lined
path led from its entryway to a small dock. Behind the
house, a formal garden sat between it and outbuildings
including a bakehouse, an office, and a barn large
enough to hold a dozen horses.

While the house was under construction, Penn lived in Philadelphia. From there he set about establishing the colony he had dreamed of. As the proprietor of a vast territory, he had much work to do. His first tasks were to establish good relations with the leaders of nearby colonies and to cement good relations with the Native American inhabitants of Pennsylvania.

In early November he traveled to New York and East Jersey to meet with the leaders of those colonies. It is believed that not long after his return to Pennsylvania, he met with Indian leaders to conclude what has come to be known as the Great Treaty. According to legend, this meeting took place under a large elm tree in a place called Shackamaxon. The Indians, so the legend goes, pledged themselves to "live in love with William Penn and his children so long as the Sun and the Moon shall endure."[3]

A famous painting by the American artist Benjamin West shows this meeting between Penn and the Native American leaders. However, the painting was made long after Penn's death, and it is filled with historical inaccuracies. In the painting's background, West shows several large brick buildings that weren't in existence in Philadelphia in 1682. He portrays the Quakers as stern and the Indians as subservient and pictures Penn as a potbellied, middle-aged man. In truth, the few houses in Philadelphia at that time were small, wooden structures. The Indians, far from being subservient, were proud chiefs. Penn and the other Quakers would have met them in friendship, sitting on the ground as they discussed the terms of the agreement. And Penn, at that time, was a relatively young man of thirty-eight, tall and strong and fit enough to engage in foot races with the Indian braves.

"William Penn's Treaty with the Indians." The original oil painting by Benjamin West is now on display in Independence Hall in Philadelphia.

While some historians doubt that Penn ever met with the Indian leaders under the Shackamaxon Elm, there is no reason to doubt that such a meeting took place. Indeed, Indians spoke of the treaty for generations after Penn's death. A wampum belt showing a hatted man holding the hand of an Indian, said to have been given to Penn by the Native Americans in honor of the treaty, is today preserved at the Historical Society of Pennsylvania.

Did Penn and the Indians actually meet under the Shackamaxon Elm? The great French philosopher Voltaire, who was a young man of twenty when Penn died, wrote of the Great Treaty as if it was a historical fact. It was, he said, the "only treaty between [the Indians] and the Christians which was never sworn to and never broken."[4]

Whether the story of the treaty is true or not, it is a fact that Penn treated the native inhabitants of Pennsylvania with respect and even love. He traveled to their villages without guards and, of course, unarmed, relying on their goodness for protection. He learned their language and often visited them in their homes. As a Christian and a good Quaker, he hoped to convert the Native Americans to the Christian religion, but he respected their beliefs. As a result, he was loved and respected by the Native Americans of Pennsylvania who called him *Onas*, an Indian word meaning "pen" or "quill."

During this time, Penn was also busy setting the colony's government in motion. In early December, the first meeting of the colony's voters was held in Chester. While only about half the settlers attended that meeting, they quickly approved the draft of the constitution that Penn had written a year earlier, with just a few small modifications.

Following that meeting, Penn traveled south to meet with Lord Baltimore, the grandson of Maryland's founder. The boundary between Pennsylvania and Maryland had not been clearly defined when Penn's charter was granted, and now both Penn and Baltimore were claiming the western bank of the Delaware from about New Castle south. This land was important to Pennsylvania since it gave the province direct access to Delaware Bay. In Maryland, Penn argued that the settlers needed access to the bay and the sea beyond. Try as hard as he could, though, he could not convince Baltimore to give up his claim to the land. The meeting between the two proprietors accomplished nothing other than an agreement to meet again at a later date.

Penn had little time to devote to the conflict between Pennsylvania and Maryland. Ships were arriving from England at the rate of about one each week. Each ship carried new settlers—men, women, and children who were Penn's responsibility. These settlers came long before land was cleared or houses were built. They lived as best they could, often camping under the great trees that stood shoulder to shoulder in the forests or in caves dug in the soft banks along the river.

From Penn's point of view, giving the settlers the power to control their own destinies involved more than simply seeing to it that they were housed. He wanted to put the reins of government in the hands of people as quickly as possible. Not long after returning from his visit to Baltimore, he called for the election of officers to serve as the colony's first assembly. "Let all that is done be the act of the people and so it will be safe," he said in a letter to Markham.[5]

On March 10, 1683, the first session of the newly elected assembly met at Philadelphia. At that time, a new Frame of Government was created. While very much like the Frame of Government written by Penn in England, this new document contained some changes. It was amended to include the three southern counties that made up what is now the state of Delaware; it reduced the size of the council to eighteen members and of the assembly to thirty-six. It also gave voters the right to elect sheriffs, justices of the peace, and coroners.

During these early months, as Penn dealt with the thousands of details involved in founding and governing a colony, Philadelphia and the region around it thrived. By the end of the summer of 1683, eighty houses—many of brick, with large balconies—stood in the City of Brotherly Love where just ten had stood when Penn arrived in Pennsylvania. Other colonists built large estates on the riverbanks not far from the city.

Meanwhile, Penn received news that Guli, who was expecting a child when he set sail from Deal, had given birth to a daughter in the spring of 1683. In early April, a Quaker named James Claypoole wrote to Penn with the news that he had seen the baby and that all was well. ". . . my wife and I . . . came to thy house . . . where we were very kindly entertained by thy dear wife and stayed until the 26th [of March] and then came away," Claypoole reported. "She and thy four children were in good health."[6]

Sadly, Claypoole's letter was followed almost immediately by the distressing news that the baby had died when she was just three weeks old.

Penn had little time to mourn the death of the child he had never seen. He continued overseeing the establishment of the colony as shiploads of Irish, English, Scottish, and German immigrants flocked to Pennsylvania. He directed the construction of Pennsbury and went on several trips exploring the far reaches of his colony. On those journeys, he met Native American leaders, purchased land, and further strengthened the good relations he was building with the Indians.

During those months, Penn continued to be troubled by the unresolved dispute with Lord Baltimore. It was becoming increasingly clear to Penn that the dispute would have to be resolved by the authorities in England.

At the same time, Penn was troubled by the knowledge that some settlers were violating the English law known as the Navigation Acts by trading with non-British merchants and by engaging in smuggling. Such activities, he knew, could give unfriendly lawmakers in England ammunition they needed to remove the colony from Penn's control and out of the hands of the Quakers.

If those troubles were not sufficient, Penn was also worried about money. He had spent a small fortune, more than six thousand pounds, to obtain his charter and to finance the province during its first year. In return, he had not earned so much as a shilling. In desperation, he asked the assembly to authorize the early payment of some of the rents he was due on lands he sold to colonists. The assembly, probably because its members viewed him as a wealthy man, refused. In fact, his request for money started grumbling on the part of some colonists that for all his high-and-mighty talk, he was no better than a greedy hypocrite. These early problems with settlers set a pattern that was to be unbroken during the remainder of Penn's life.

In the midst of these troubles, in May 1684, Penn received word that Lord Baltimore and his family were leaving Maryland for England. Penn knew the Maryland proprietor was on his way to argue his case before the king's Privy Council, who might rule in Baltimore's favor.

As quickly as he could, Penn prepared for his own departure. He left the control of the colony's government in the hands of the council under the leadership of a Quaker named Thomas Lloyd and turned responsibility for the construction and management of Pennsbury over to a steward, James Harrison. He wrote a letter to Guli advising her that he was on his way to England. Worried that he might die at sea, he wrote a will in which he left large plots of land to Guli and each of his children. Guli was also to inherit Pennsbury until Springett came of age, at which time it would become his manor. In the event of his death, fifty thousand acres of land was to be given at no cost to poor families. An additional forty thousand acres were set aside to be used for schools and hospitals.

On August 12, Penn set sail for England aboard the ketch *Endeavour*. The Pennsylvania he left behind had some seven thousand residents, many of whom had come in the three years since he received his charter. Philadelphia boasted a population of about twenty-five hundred persons, who had built more than three hundred and fifty dwellings. As Penn stood looking over the ship's rail he felt proud of what he had accomplished. But his pride was, in his words, "without vanity."[7] God, after all, had guided him and helped him in founding his colony. "My God," he said, "hath given [Pennsylvania] me. . . ."[8]

As the ketch made its way downriver to the sea, William Penn felt sadness at leaving the place he regarded as home. His love of Pennsylvania was obvious in a letter he wrote to the City of Philadelphia: "My love and my life is to you, and with you: and no water can quench it, nor distance wear it out, or bring it to an end. I have been with you, cared over you and served you with unfeigned love; and you are beloved of me."[9]

He had no way of knowing that it would be fifteen years before he saw his beloved province again.

TWELVE

A Day to Be Wise

Penn arrived in England on October 6, 1684. Immediately, he rushed to Worminghurst to be with the beloved family he had not seen in more than two years. His heart must have filled with joy as he embraced Guli, nine-year-old Springett, six-year-old Letitia, and little William Jr., who had been just an infant when Penn departed for Pennsylvania two years earlier.

Sadly, that joy was short-lived. He was only at Worminghurst a few hours when he realized that one of his assistants in Pennsylvania had neglected to pack important documents he needed to argue his case in the land dispute with Lord Baltimore. Though Penn was nonviolent, he did have a temper. His anger over this mistake was evident in a letter he immediately sent to Pennsylvania, asking that the papers be posted to him as quickly as possible. "I am now here with my finger in my mouth," he said.[1]

Luckily for Penn, the hearing to determine the ownership of the disputed land was delayed, first at the request of the commissioners of the Board of Trade

and Plantations and then again at the request of Lord
Baltimore.

Soon after his return to England, Penn visited
Charles II and James, the duke of York. He found the
king and his brother, he said, "sour and stern, and resolved to hold the reins of power with a stiffer hand
than heretofore."[2]

In fact, the situation for the Quakers and other dissenters in England had grown much worse while Penn
was in America. The king was being challenged by Parliament and by political liberals, called Whigs, who
wanted to curb his power. Charles reacted to the threat
to his rule like a tyrant. He attacked religious and political dissenters. Many Whigs were imprisoned, and
not a few were executed, including Penn's old friend
Algernon Sidney. Nonconformist meetinghouses were
destroyed, dissident ministers were jailed, books that
were considered dangerous were burned. As always,
the Quakers were easy targets, and at the time Penn
returned to England some fourteen hundred Friends
were in prison throughout Britain.

Though Penn was a friend of both Charles and the
duke of York, he knew he had to stand up for the imprisoned Quakers. At the same time, he knew he had
to proceed carefully or he might endanger Pennsylvania or find himself jailed or hanged. Deciding to act
with subtlety, he wrote a manuscript he called *True Interest of King and Kingdom,* in which he advised Charles
to act with moderation, not to tear England apart in
the interests of protecting her. Instead of publishing
the manuscript, he sent it to the king for his review,
obviously hoping that it might convince Charles to stop
his persecution of the Friends and other dissidents.

It is not certain if Charles II ever read Penn's manuscript or if he planned to take the Quaker's advice, for, on February 1, 1685, the king suffered a stroke. In a letter to Friends in Pennsylvania, Penn described what happened: "He was well on . . . the first of February; about eight next morning, as he sat down to shave, his head twitched both ways . . . , and he gave a shriek, and fell as dead."

Incapacitated by the stroke he suffered that morning, Charles was treated by physicians who, with the best medical knowledge then available, "blooded him and cupped him, and plied his head with red-hot frying pans."[3] Draining the king's blood and applying heated glass cups to his chest and back and red-hot iron plates to his head—all designed to lower his blood pressure and remove "bad" blood from his body—did no good. On February 6, Charles II died and the duke of York ascended the throne as King James II.

Penn had come to London to protect his colony's borders. Now that James was king, he hoped he could do much more for his province, for Quakers, and for other nonconformists. He knew that the new king would move to end the persecution of Catholics and hoped that he could convince his old friend and the friend of his father to end the persecution of all religious dissenters. His hopes were buoyed at a meeting he had with James soon after Charles's death. At that meeting, when Penn asked about toleration for Quakers, James "smiled, and said he desired not that peaceable people should be disturbed for their religion."[4]

James was as good as his word. Within weeks of his coronation on April 23, 1685, he issued a limited declaration of toleration, ending some of the worst of the persecution. Penn was ecstatic. Few in the kingdom knew better than he did how widespread such persecution was. He himself had been arrested three times for attendance at Quaker meetings in the weeks between his arrival in England and the death of Charles. Now, finally, it appeared that Quakers and other dissenters might find true tolerance in their own land.

The very next month, though, those hopes were shattered when the duke of Monmouth, one of the illegitimate sons of King Charles II, led a rebellion to wrest the crown from James II. Though the Monmouth rebellion was quickly put down, reprisals against dissenters were long and bloody. Only a handful of Quakers were punished, since they had not taken part in the uprising, but hopes for real religious freedom were dashed.

Penn found himself walking the political equivalent of a tightrope. It was, he said in a letter to a Friend in Pennsylvania, "a day to be wise."[5] On the one hand, Penn opposed the bloody persecutions taking place throughout the kingdom. On the other hand, he knew he could not risk losing Pennsylvania by openly opposing the king. During these times, Penn visited with James almost every day. Dressed in his plain Quaker garb, with his hat firmly clamped on his head, he mingled with the dandies of the court in their silks and satins. From all accounts, the king and Penn truly had warm feelings for each other. James respected Penn for his plainspoken ways and, no doubt, for his loyalty at a time when the Crown was under attack.

Penn's continuing friendship for James, the instigator of the bloody persecutions, is harder to understand. It appears, though, that Penn believed that the persecutions were more the work of Sir George Jeffreys, the lord chief justice who was in charge of punishing dissenters, than they were of the king. James II, he once said, was "hurried into all this effusion of blood by Jeffreys' impetuous and cruel temper."[6] Then, too, Penn knew that his continuing friendship with the king represented the best hope the Quakers and other dissenters had for ever obtaining freedom of conscience. Only by remaining friendly with the king could he continue arguing with the ruler in favor of toleration.

Soon, Penn and James were spending "not one but many hours together."[7] The friendship between the Quaker and the king led to rumors that Penn himself was a Catholic, or even a priest who had been given a dispensation to marry by the Pope himself. Some rumormongers even said that Penn always wore a hat to hide the fact that his hair was cut in a tonsure, like a monk's.

In late 1685, meanwhile, the border dispute between Penn and Lord Baltimore was at least partially resolved when the government ruled that the territory in question should be split in half, with the half on the Delaware River going to Penn while the other half, now known as the Eastern Shore of Maryland, was awarded to Lord Baltimore. The exact border between Pennsylvania and Maryland, however, was not finally determined until many years later, long after both Penn and Lord Baltimore were dead.

With that issue resolved, Penn was torn between his desire to stay in England and his need to return to Pennsylvania. Someone, he knew, had to promote the cause of tolerance and work to gain freedom for all those hundreds of Friends still rotting in jails in Lon-

don and Bristol and other English cities. At the same
time, he was needed in Pennsylvania. Social conditions
in the province were not what he had imagined they
would be when he established his "holy experiment."
Taverns and houses where "looseness" was practiced
were common in Philadelphia. There was official mis-
conduct among some of the men elected to the assembly and almost ceaseless arguing between Quaker and
non-Quaker factions in government. All these problems in Pennsylvania were gleefully reported to officials in England by men who were opposed to Penn's
ownership of the colony. These reports could easily
convince the English government to take control of
the province. "Cannot more friendly and private
courses be taken to set matters to rights in an infant
province whose steps are . . . watched," he wrote to
the men he had left in charge. "For the love of God,
me and the poor country, be not so governmentish; so
noisy and open, in your disaffections."[8]

At the same time, Penn's money worries had grown
worse. Rents due him from settlers were not being paid.
His Irish estates were not producing the income he had
expected. Since he was spending so much time at the
Court, he had taken lodgings in London, spacious
rooms that could house himself and his family. That
meant he was paying expenses for two households, in
addition to the cost of building Pennsbury. He was
forced to plead with the officials in Pennsylvania to
send him money, and when none was sent, he had to
sell land belonging to Guli to pay his living expenses.

Ultimately, Penn decided to stay in England to fight
for religious freedom for all. He threw himself into the
battle, writing several tracts in defense of freedom of

conscience. Thanks to his work, some dissidents were freed, and others were pardoned. One who was pardoned was John Trenchard, a friend of Penn's who had fled to the Netherlands to escape persecution. Later, after his return to England, Trenchard was made chief justice of Chester. Eventually he would be in a position to do a good turn for Penn.

Meanwhile, as word spread that William Penn had influence in the Court, he began to be besieged by men and women seeking favors. Sometimes as many as two hundred people crowded around him as he made his way to the palace, each one seeking help. He managed to provide needed assistance to many of these petitioners.

Finally, he achieved one of his greatest goals when, in March 1686, King James II issued a general pardon, an order that all religious prisoners be released from jails in England. More than thirteen hundred Friends were released.

A famous Quaker historian wrote of the joy that followed that general pardon: "It was a great consolation at their ensuing Annual Meeting in London to have the company of so many valuable Friends, whose faces had not been seen there for many years, having been [held] in prison, some of them, twelve or fifteen years and upward, for no crime but endeavoring to keep a good conscience toward God."[9] Penn himself called the release of the imprisoned Quakers "something wonderful that God had wrought."[10]

At about that time, Guli gave birth to another child, a daughter the Penns named Gulielma Maria. Little Guli was sickly, as had been so many of the Penn children, but she slowly gained strength.

Following the baby's birth, with the Quakers free from jail, Penn could have returned to Pennsylvania, taking Guli and the children with him. In spite of the king's general pardon, however, the laws against nonconformists were still in force. Penn decided to stay to work for the repeal of those laws.

In the spring of 1687, it appeared that goal was achieved when King James II suspended laws against nonconformists. Unfortunately, he took those steps on his own, without seeking the approval of the elected members of Parliament, as required by the law of the land. As far as Parliament and most of the people of England were concerned, James's actions were like waving a red flag in front of a bull. Penn, who should have been overjoyed, saw danger ahead for James. He quickly led a deputation of Quakers to Whitehall, the king's palace, to thank his friend, but he said in his speech that he hoped the Parliament would agree to the king's actions.

That mistake by King James was followed by another. He tried to force Magdalen College of Oxford University—one of the kingdom's most Protestant institutions—to accept a Catholic as its head. Then, in the spring of 1688, James went even further, issuing a second Declaration of Indulgence, reaffirming the first, and ordering ministers to read the declaration in churches throughout the kingdom. In the wake of this action, seven bishops of the Anglican Church asked James to withdraw the order. Like a man bent on his own destruction, the king had the bishops arrested on charges of treason.

The English people, most of whom were Anglican, were distressed to see their church abused in this way.

Still, up to this time, James could have avoided tragedy. There was nothing he had done that could not be easily undone.

Then, in June 1688, a son, James Edward, was born to King James and his queen.

Until that time, the Protestant English were reassured by the knowledge that Mary of Orange, James's Protestant daughter, was heir to the throne. After all, James was a relatively old man, all of fifty-three, when he was crowned. Someday—soon, perhaps—he would die and England would again be under Protestant rule. With the birth of a male heir who would certainly be raised as a Catholic, however, all that changed. A group of the most powerful men in England met and composed a letter to William of Orange, Mary's husband. In that letter, they invited him to come to England, with his army, to depose their king and make England his to rule.

On November 5, 1688, William of Orange landed with an army of fourteen thousand men on the coast of Devon. Within weeks, the king and his family were forced to flee from England, leaving the throne to the joint rule of his daughter and son-in-law. What has come to be known as the Glorious Revolution changed the course of English history. It also changed the course of William Penn's life. The Quaker founder of Pennsylvania was about to find himself surrounded by storms of trouble and controversy which would last more than a decade and strip from him much of what he had fought for all his life.

THIRTEEN

A Man of Sorrow

Suddenly William Penn, for years a favorite at the Court and a confidant of the king, was an outsider. With his old friend James in exile, the rumors that he was a secret Catholic—a Jesuit—were replaced by even more dangerous rumors that he was a so-called Jacobite, a supporter of James who would commit treason to see his friend restored to the throne. He was, in late 1688, in danger of losing his liberty, if not his life.

Penn could have fled from England, as hundreds of former supporters of James did. Instead, he stayed in London, determined to continue working for his province and certain that those who studied his life would be convinced of his loyalty to England. Indeed, he was so confident of his safety that he continued visiting Whitehall, now the palace of William and Mary, in hopes of pleading the Quaker case to the new king.

Penn's reasoning was optimistic. On December 10, 1688, he was taken into custody and dragged before the king's Privy Council for questioning to determine his loyalty. In response to questions, he told the king's advisors that he "loved his country and the Protestant religion above his life."[1] Though he was soon released, he was ordered to post a bond of six thousand pounds and to stand trial on charges of being a Jacobite. At that trial, in March 1689, he was acquitted of any wrongdoing.

Penn was arrested twice more during the next eighteen months. Each time he was questioned and ultimately freed, for there was never any proof that he was a traitor. He might have made his own life easier if he had not been so faithful to his old friend James. Instead, he displayed the loyalty that was always a hallmark of his life. Once, when he was questioned by William II, he said he had always "loved King James," and, "as he loved him in his prosperity he could not hate him in his adversity." Such love, Penn added, did not mean he was willing to commit treason.[2]

In 1689, even as Penn was being politically persecuted, Quakers finally gained a measure of religious freedom when King William signed the Act of Toleration. Thanks to this act, Quakers and other Protestant dissenters were free to meet for religious services. The act also made it possible for Quakers to substitute an affirmation, or solemn promise, in place of an oath. The passage of this act was in a real sense a victory for Penn, who had so passionately argued for freedom for so many years. It was also a victory for Quakers who had spilled their blood and lost their freedom in resistance to persecution.

While Penn was cheered by the passage of the Act of Toleration, there was little other good news in his life at that time. Virtually no rents were being realized from his estates in Ireland or from Pennsylvania. Indeed, all the news from his colony was bad. The colony's government was in disarray, torn by disagreements that arose as Pennsylvania's population grew and non-Quaker immigrants flowed into the lands along the Delaware. Elected officials in the province were unable to deal with the conflicts. Even from a distance, Penn saw that his dream of a "holy experiment" that would stand as an example to the world was not being realized. In 1688, Penn, under siege in England and beset by money worries, apparently forgot his own belief that the people would be happiest when they were ruled democratically. He named John Blackwell, a non-Quaker and a strict, hard-bitten man as his lieutenant governor. Hoping that Blackwell would be able to force the settlers to pay him the back rents he desperately needed, he told the former soldier: "Rule the meek meekly, and those that will not be ruled, rule with authority."[3] Blackwell took him at his word and, from his first days in Pennsylvania, he offended the Quakers in the province. Finally, Penn asked Blackwell for his resignation and instructed the assembly to nominate five men as candidates for governor. From that list, he would choose the name of one who would rule the colony in his absence.

During these years, as Penn was in danger of losing his colony, hounded by the law, realizing no profits from his Pennsylvania venture, he and Guli and his children were able to be together only rarely in lodgings he had taken in Hammersmith, a small village on the banks of the Thames. There, on November 20, 1689, personal tragedy was added to his other woes when his youngest child, four-year-old Gulielma Maria, died. She was buried in the Jordans Meeting House graveyard near the graves of the firstborn Gulielma and the twins.

Finally, in late 1690, Penn decided it was time to return to Pennsylvania. Having been tried three times for treason and acquitted each time, he was convinced his name had been adequately cleared. The Act of Toleration guaranteed English Friends at least some freedoms. He had, he thought, done all he could do in the land of his birth.

Penn quickly made arrangements for his journey. He obtained a ship that would carry him and his family to the Delaware, and arranged for a government convoy to guard the vessel on its crossing to America.

In the midst of these preparations, Penn and the Quaker movement suffered a great loss when George Fox suddenly fell ill and died. Penn was with Fox on January 13, 1691, when, at about nine-thirty at night, the Quaker founder breathed his last. As Fox's friend, he was given the responsibility of writing of the founder's death to his widow, Margaret. "I am to be the teller to thee of sorrowful tidings . . . ," he wrote. ". . . Thy dear husband and my beloved and dear friend G. Fox, has finished his glorious testimony this night. . . . My soul is deeply affected with this hasty great loss. . . ."[4]

Penn was also chosen to speak a memorial to Fox at the burial ground. It was only luck that kept him from being arrested yet again as he spoke in remembrance of Fox, for magistrates showed up at the graveyard just moments after the burial ended. This time, Penn's trouble stemmed from the testimony of a man named William Fuller, who swore an oath in Ireland that Penn was involved in a plot against the Crown. Fuller later was convicted and sentenced for perjury, but at the time of Fox's death his word was good enough that a warrant was issued for Penn's arrest on charges of treason.

As soon as Penn heard of the warrant he knew he would never obtain justice in England. He knew that if he gave himself up to answer the charges against him, he would be faced in court by Fuller, a liar who would happily swear he was telling the truth. He, on the other hand, would speak the truth, but would be unable to swear an oath. Even if he was somehow acquitted, he would only be arrested again. He decided to hide in London until he could convince William and Mary of his innocence once and for all.

Soon after the warrant was issued for his arrest, Penn wrote an epistle (an open letter) to the Quakers in Europe and the New World. In that letter he stated his case simply. ". . . Of one thing be assured," he said, "I am innocent. . . ."[5]

As the ship he had arranged for the voyage to Pennsylvania set sail without him and his family, Guli and the children moved back to Worminghurst. Penn dropped out of sight. His hiding place was known only to his family and a few close and trusted friends.

It was to be three years before Penn would be able to walk a free man again. In these years he saw Guli only a few times. Growing older and never very strong, she was worn down by her husband's troubles.

Though he was in hiding, Penn was not without resources. He still had friends in high places. He wrote several letters asking those friends to intercede on his behalf with King William. Several letters were sent to Henry Sidney, the earl of Romney and the younger brother of Penn's old friend Algernon Sidney. "Lay my case before [the King]," Penn pleaded, "And God almighty dispose him to . . . allow me to live quietly anywhere, either in this kingdom or in America. . . . I will make no ill use of his favor." Romney was persuaded to intercede on Penn's behalf and told the king that Penn was a "true and faithful servant. . . ."[6]

Through Romney and others, Penn begged for a chance to meet with the king. He knew he could convince the monarch of his innocence if only he could speak with him, face to face, as he did in 1689. William refused to meet with him. The days of Penn's easy access to the Crown were over.

At the same time, not much of an attempt was made to capture Penn. In all likelihood, the king and queen were happy he was out of circulation, unable to speak in public or cause problems. They probably also wanted to avoid having to place such a well-known figure, with thousands of supporters, on trial.

During this period of forced solitude and separation from those he loved, Penn's troubles mounted. The news from Pennsylvania was bad. The upper counties and lower counties argued about the form of government they wanted in the province. There were disagreements about whether the colony should provide military aid to the English in the French and Indian War, which started in 1689. The Quakers were torn by dissent over religious matters. And he could do nothing.

Perhaps the worst news to reach Penn in those days concerned Maryland, where internal disputes led the king's Privy Council to take the province under its protection, to make it a royal province. With its owner charged with treason and its government torn by dissent, the same thing could happen to Pennsylvania.

In September 1691, Penn wrote a letter to the council in Philadelphia that clearly showed his unhappiness. "I am a man of sorrows," he said, "and you [increase] my griefs, not because you don't love me, but because you don't love one another."[7]

Penn was desperate and almost destitute. In the years since James fell from power, his Irish estates had been ravaged by war between forces loyal to James and those loyal to William. They had, in recent years, provided him with almost no income. Now, under formal charges of treason, those lands and the little rent they produced were taken by the Crown. Rents from Pennsylvania also were almost nonexistent. Penn pleaded with the settlers in Philadelphia. Could not one hundred persons in the city lend him one hundred pounds each for four years, interest free? During that time, he would surely be able to return to Pennsylvania, bringing hundreds of new settlers. His plea for financial aid was never answered.

The worst blow, however, was struck in the summer of 1692. At that time, King William took Pennsylvania away from Penn and put it under the rule of Governor Benjamin Fletcher of New York. In reality, the move to make Pennsylvania a royal province was not so much against Penn as it was to help England in her war with France. England needed her colonies united to present a strong defensive wall to the French, who had spread all along the Mississippi Valley. Pacifist Pennsylvania, unwilling to provide soldiers or funds to the English army, was a weak spot in that defensive wall.

Penn's troubles were, by this time, overwhelming. His enemies had the upper hand. He was forced to live in hiding. The very people he had helped escape from persecution turned their backs on him in his time of need. He was poor, separated from his loving wife and children. And now Pennsylvania, his beloved colony, was taken from him.

Penn could have given up. Instead, he picked up his quill pen and wrote some of the most powerful, moving, enduring words of his life. Uppermost in his mind was the fact that his colony was now embroiled, at least peripherally, in a territorial war in America. He therefore looked at the problems of the militant world and found a solution.

William Penn's *An Essay Towards the Present and Future Peace of Europe*, proposed a union of European nations dedicated to preserving freedom, justice, and peace. "He must not be a man, but a statue of brass or stone, [who does] not melt when he beholds the bloody tragedies of . . . war," he wrote.[8] Peace, he argued, is a product of justice. Justice is a product of governments that act in accordance with moral laws. And moral governments are the products of free societies.

He proposed that the rulers of Europe, "for the . . . love of peace and order," would send ambassadors to regular meetings of a group to be called the "Parliament of Europe." At these meetings, differences would be resolved so that war could be avoided.[9]

Today, Penn's ideas seem ordinary. More than three hundred years ago, when nationalism was rampant and nation-states were fighting bitterly for territory, they were remarkable. Sadly, Penn's proposal for a "Parliament of Europe" was cast aside until relatively modern times, when his ideas took form in the League of Nations and the United Nations.

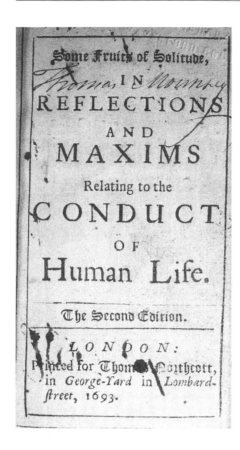

The title page of the second edition of Penn's work Some Fruits of Solitude

The other great work written by Penn in those years in hiding is a short book he called *Some Fruits of Solitude*. This is a book of "reflections and maxims" relating to the conduct of life. It is a little book filled with riches. One of many people who read it and loved it was Robert Louis Stevenson, the famous writer. "I carried [it] in my pocket all about the San Francisco streets, read in street-cars and ferry-boats . . . and found in all times and places a peaceful and sweet companion. . . . There is not the man living—no, nor recently dead—

that could put . . . so much honest, kind wisdom into words," Stevenson said.[10]

Here are a few of Penn's maxims:

> They have a right to censure, that have a Heart to help: the rest is cruelty, not Justice.

> Men are generally more careful of the Breed of their Horses and Dogs than of their Children.

> There can be no friendship where there is no Freedom.

> It is wise not to seek a secret, and honest not to reveal one.

> God is better served by resisting a Temptation to Evil, than in many formal prayers.[11]

Nowhere in this book, written when Penn was at what had to be the low point of a life filled with pain and struggles, is there a hint of bitterness. Instead, as he labored alone, in hiding, he "blesseth God for his Retirement, and kisses the Gentle Hand which led him into it."[12] In the Quaker way, Penn accepted his misfortune as his God's will and put it to good use.

Though he accepted his circumstances, he did not sit idly by waiting for them to change. He continued, in those months, writing to Friends in Europe and America. Finally, in late 1693, several of his friends at Court went to William and asked for the favor of Penn's release. The case against him, they said, had been based on the testimony of a liar. They had known Penn, they told the king, for many years, and had never known him to do anything evil. On the contrary, they all had known him to do good not just for the Quakers but for

England herself. King William agreed and said word should be brought to Penn that he was a free man, exonerated of all charges against him. He would, the king added, see to it that the news of Penn's freedom was given to Sir John Trenchard, by that time England's secretary of state.

This was the same John Trenchard whom Penn had helped years before. Now Sir John sent word to Penn to visit him in his home. There he gave Penn the news he had been waiting to hear. Penn was a free man and would remain free so long as he lived quietly and prudently.

Penn's first act after getting word of his exoneration was to go, with his son Springett, to a nearby Quaker meeting. There he settled into a seat, in silence and comfort, surrounded by Friends for the first time in almost four years.

After the meeting, he hurried to be with Guli, Tish, and Billy. As soon as Penn saw his wife, he knew she was very ill. Though she was relatively young at the age of forty-nine, Guli looked much older. Always weak, she had been worn down by worry and by the rigors of caring for the family with her husband in hiding. Penn, though, hoped that his return would help her get better. "My wife is yet weakly," he wrote to Friends in Pennsylvania in mid-January 1694, "but I am not without hopes of her recovery, who is . . . the best of wives and women. . . ."[13]

Penn's hopes for her recovery were in vain. On February 23, 1694, Gulielma Springett Penn died, in her husband's arms, with her head cradled against his chest. "She was not only an excellent wife and mother, but an entire and constant friend. [Her death] was our great loss . . ." Penn said.[14]

FOURTEEN

Emergence from the Shadows

Following his wife's death, Penn fell into a deep depression. He and his beloved Guli had been married for twenty-two years. She had been not only his wife and friend, but also a witness and helper during his coming-of-age as a Quaker leader. During this period of sadness, he even found it difficult to put pen to paper, complaining in a letter to an American Friend that his sadness made him "unfit to write much."[1]

Not surprisingly, Penn found relief in the company of his fellow Quakers. Slowly, as he regained his strength, he began visiting meetings. He started writing again, though not with the same intensity as before. In this period, he wrote a preface to George Fox's Journal, reprinted as *A Brief Account of the Rise and Progress of the People Called Quakers*. In this work, he outlined the fundamental principles and beliefs of the Quakers and paid tribute to the great Quaker founder.

During these months, the troubles in Pennsylvania continued. Benjamin Fletcher, the man who was put in charge of the colony after it was taken from Penn, found it difficult to get the colonists to provide the military assistance he needed to protect New York in the ongoing war with the French and Indians. At this time, Penn saw an opportunity to regain his proprietorship.

In the summer of 1694, he petitioned the Lords Commissioners of Trade and Plantations for restoration of the charter that had been taken from him while he was in hiding. He still had high-ranking friends at Whitehall, and he asked them for help. The Lords Commissioners were willing to return the province to Penn's ownership and care. In order to get it back, though, he had to promise that he would personally return to Pennsylvania to serve as its governor and guarantee that Pennsylvania would provide eighty men annually for the defense of the English colonies or pay the cost of eighty replacement soldiers.

The first requirement posed no hardship. He was happy to promise he would return to the lands on the Delaware. The second—to provide soldiers—must have caused much soul-searching. After all, he was a Quaker, pledged to nonviolence. He recognized, however, that there was no alternative and that England could force the colony to contribute men or money. In mid-August, he assured the Crown that he intended "with all convenient speed to repair [to Pennsylvania] and take care of the government and provide for the safety and surety thereof."[2] On August 20, a royal grant issued by King William and Queen Mary returned the administration of the province and its territories to Penn.

Penn wanted to return to Pennsylvania immediately, but was still forced to put off his departure from England. His finances were still in terrible shape. Though his Irish estates had been returned to him following his exoneration by King William, they still were not producing much in the way of rent. And though he had spent many thousands of pounds to finance and support his province of Pennsylvania, he continued to be unable to collect rents that were legally his due. He had asked for help from the wealthy settlers in Philadelphia and been turned down. No, his return would have to wait, at least for a time, until he found some way to get needed cash. In the meantime, he appointed William Markham to once again serve as his deputy governor in the province.

As he tried to arrange his departure, Penn resumed his active role in Quaker affairs in England. Older now, seasoned by personal loss and sufferings, he was a popular speaker. With Springett at his side, he traveled from meeting to meeting in the west of England. Wherever he went, large crowds turned out to hear him speak. Sometime in late 1694, he visited Bristol, the seaside city that had been the birthplace of his father. There, after a meeting at which he spoke to a large crowd of Friends, he met Hannah Callowhill, the unmarried thirty-year-old daughter of one of the city's leading Quaker families.

Penn was no stranger to Bristol, and almost certainly no stranger to Thomas Callowhill or to his wife or daughter, Hannah. He had been in the city several times, and gone to meetings there on several occasions. Now, though, he saw Hannah as a woman he might marry. He was fifty-five years old, and he needed a wife for himself and a mother for his children. He began courting the much-younger Hannah, extending his stay in Bristol just as he had at Amersham so many years before when he was courting Guli.

By mid-January 1695, Penn was back at Worming-hurst. From there, he wooed Hannah in an almost businesslike manner. He wrote letters not only to her, but to her mother and father as well. He sent a recipe for drying fruit to Mrs. Callowhill and let Thomas Callowhill know that he could call on him at any time for legal help or advice.

Hannah, meanwhile, resisted his courtship, at least so long as it was conducted through the mail. In one letter to her, written in September 1695, he said: "I behold, love and value thee and desire, above all other considerations, to be . . . esteemed by thee. . . . I would persuade myself thou art of the same mind, tho' it is hard to make thee say so. Yet that must come in time. . . . the time draws near, in which I shall enforce this subject beyond all [argument]."[3]

To plead his case in person, Penn visited Bristol sometime in October. Accompanying him on this journey were Springett, Letitia, and young Billy. The pledge of love that he could not win from Hannah in writing, he won once they were together. Within a few weeks they were busily making wedding plans, seeking approval from her meeting in Bristol and his in Sussex.

Penn soon returned to Worminghurst, and letters flew between his house and hers. Penn wasn't the only one who wrote. His daughter Letitia, who was then about eighteen years old, sent a charming letter in which she assured Hannah of her father's love. "I must tell thee," she said, "that at my father's first coming from Bristol ten months [earlier] . . . I perceived . . . he had entertained an inward and deep affection for thee, by the character he gave of thee, and pleasure he took to recommend thee for an example to others." Because of that, she added, she had been anxious to meet Hannah in Bristol. "I am sure I was not disappointed," she added, "for ever since my esteem for thee has increased, and my father's [plan] been more and more pleasant to me."[4]

As Penn and Hannah made plans for their wedding, illness, probably influenza, struck the Penn household and the community around it. Billy, then about fifteen, was the first to get sick, followed quickly by his father. Letitia seems to have avoided the illness, as did Springett, at least for a time, but Billy grew worse. Penn, meanwhile, complained that he was ill and "much fallen away," or losing weight.[5]

In February, Springett fell ill, but by that time the others had recovered, and his illness did not keep the family from traveling to Bristol. There, on March 5, 1696, William Penn and Hannah Callowhill joined hands in the Quaker marriage ceremony. Sixty-six names were signed to the marriage certificate, including those of three members of Guli's family, indicating that the match was approved by his first wife's relatives.

Hannah Penn's first task as William's wife was caring for twenty-one-year-old Springett, who grew sicker in the days immediately following the marriage. As the days passed, it became obvious to all, including Springett himself, that he was deathly ill. On April 10, 1696, between nine and ten in the morning, Springett, Penn's eldest child, died.

With the boy's death, Penn said he "lost all that any father can lose in a child, since he was capable of anything that became a sober young man; my friend and companion, as well as most affectionate and dutiful child."[6]

Hannah Callowhill Penn

As he had done following Guli's death, Penn eased his sorrow by working, writing, going to meeting after meeting. In the year following Springett's death, he published a tract about the faith and practices of the Quakers as well as a book of nine sermons preached by himself and three other Quaker speakers.

Later that year, with the same kind of vision he had shown when he proposed a European Parliament, Penn put forward a proposal for a unified government for the English colonies in America. He suggested that two deputies or representatives be appointed by each province, to meet once a year in a congress where the delegates would "debate and resolve of such measures as are most advisable for their better understanding and the public tranquility and safety. . . . Their business shall be to hear and adjust all matters of complaint or differences between province and province."[7] The congress, he explained, would make it easier for colonies to trade among themselves, standardize currency and court procedures, fight crime, and provide for the common defense.

The Lords Commissioners of Trade and Plantations, the men responsible for colonial affairs, read Penn's plan and quickly forgot it. As far as they were concerned, it sounded too much like a plan for self-government. For almost a century Penn's ideas for a colonial union were forgotten until they were resurrected by a group of revolutionaries, including Thomas Jefferson, and turned into the Constitution of the United States of America.

Penn was also kept busy, in those months and years, dealing with continuing troubles in Pennsylvania. Markham, once again serving as Penn's representative in the province, was no more able to deal with dissension among the provincial officials than Fletcher. There were also reports that he refused to take action against pirates and smugglers, and rumors he was taking bribes. Penn knew he had to find a way to return to his colony, not only to deal with the problems there but also to fulfill the promise he had made to William and Mary to speedily return to his province. All he needed was the funds.

Desperate, Penn visited Ireland in early 1698, hoping he could find tenants for the lands that had been restored to him after he was cleared of charges of treason. What he found as he surveyed the estate near Cork was disheartening. The war to restore James to the throne had torn Ireland apart. His fields, left untended, had been stripped by roving bands of soldiers, turned into wasteland. The estate he loved, he said, was "almost ruined." There was no hope it would provide him with enough money to meet his needs.[8] There was no hope, he knew, of restoring his financial health before returning to Pennsylvania. He would have to simply arrange his affairs in England the best way he could, obtain passage, and trust in God to provide for him and his family. He turned his back on Ireland and returned to England to prepare for departure.

The preparations for his second voyage to Pennsylvania took almost a full year, with time out to attend the marriage of his son and namesake, William Jr., in Bristol. By August 1699, Penn was ready to go. He probably financed this second journey to Pennsylvania by borrowing money from his new father-in-law, for Thomas Callowhill was a well-off merchant. In any case, he booked passage for himself, Hannah, and Tish and received final instructions from Whitehall. These instructions demanded that he settle the colony's affairs, end piracy and smuggling, and establish a militia for the defense of the province.

On August 18, Penn met once again with Philip Ford, his longtime business manager. By then, word had spread through Quaker circles that Ford was not to be trusted. He had been involved in questionable financial dealings with other Friends and had even taken the unheard-of step of taking other Quakers to court to obtain damages.

Penn, though, seemed not to care about reports that Ford was not always aboveboard in his business dealings. In all likelihood, the ever-loyal Penn probably chose to turn a deaf ear to the reports, preferring to remember Ford as the young man who had suffered so much for the Quaker cause, who helped him in Ireland following the death of Admiral Penn, and who helped him to make Pennsylvania a reality.

At their last meeting before Penn's departure for America, the two men discussed their financial relationship at length. This relationship had become increasingly complex and confusing over the years. Thanks to Penn's desire not to lose the province during his time in hiding, he had "sold" Pennsylvania to Ford, then "leased" it back in exchange for payments of "rent."

Now, with Penn leaving for America, Ford demanded payment in full of all money owed to him. This amounted to more than ten thousand pounds, according to his figures. There was no way Penn could meet that demand. Ford then proposed that Penn sign new papers guaranteeing the payment of the money he owed. These papers, prepared in advance by Ford and his wife, Bridget, contained explicit references to Penn's payments as rents due on the colony owned by Ford and also contained a statement that Penn had reviewed Ford's accounts and found them accurate.

The *Canterbury*, the ship that would carry Penn and his family to the Delaware, was already loaded with his household goods. Hannah was pregnant with their first child; if he delayed she might have to stay in England as Guli had done so many years before. There was no way he could miss the ship's sailing.

He signed the documents that Ford presented. "Hoping some providence might relieve me," he later said, "I subscribed."[9]

On September 3, the *Canterbury* weighed anchor. From the ship, before it sailed, Penn sent ashore a letter titled *An Epistle of Farewell to the People of God Called Quakers, Wherever Scattered or Gathered in England, Ireland, Scotland, Holland, Germany, or in Any Other Parts of Europe.* "I must leave you," he said, "but I will never forget you."[10] It was obvious he intended never to return to England, that he planned to end his days in the province he had founded. Sadly for William Penn, that was not to be the case.

FIFTEEN

America Again

The *Canterbury,* with William Penn and his family on board, reached Chester on the banks of the Delaware on December 1, 1699. Word of the proprietor's coming had preceded him to the province, and a large crowd met him as he was rowed ashore in a longboat. Settlers from New Castle, Philadelphia, and the interior mingled with Indians in excited expectation as he mounted the landing to cheers and cries of welcome.

A few exuberant young men in the crowd showed their joy by firing two shots from a cannon. In the excitement, one of them thrust a cartridge powder into the cannon's mouth before it had been properly cleaned. The cartridge exploded, and "his left hand and arm were shot in pieces."[1]

Among those on the wharf to greet Penn as the furor over the cannon shots died down was Colonel Robert Quary, the judge of the Admiralty Court posted to Pennsylvania by the English government. As Admiralty judge, he operated independently of the proprietor or of the Pennsylvania legislature. His job was to see to it that Pennsylvania obeyed English maritime law. As an ardent member of the Church of England who disliked Quakers, he was also an opponent of Penn's who wanted Pennsylvania turned into a royal province. On the day of Penn's return, though, he greeted the proprietor warmly.

The next day, Penn, his family, and his secretary, James Logan, made their way up the river to Philadelphia. The city that Penn saw upon his return bore little resemblance to the frontier town he had left in 1684. Its population now numbered five thousand, making it the second-largest city in America, behind only Boston. Most of the seven hundred homes in the city were made of brick and graced with balconies and wide porches. The gardens and parks that Penn had dreamed of so many years before dotted the cityscape. Its waterfront was a beehive of activity as ships were loaded with the province's exports of hemp, linen, lumber, whale oil, furs, tobacco, iron, and copper. Shops offered every imported luxury imaginable, and churches and schools provided care for the soul and the mind. Penn's heart must have swelled with pride and thanks to his God as he looked at the City of Brotherly Love— his city, in his province.

After landing and greeting Governor Markham, Penn and his family immediately went to the Friends' Meeting House where, since it was First Day (Sunday) he sat in communion with his God, then rose and delivered the chief sermon and prayer.

Penn knew he had to immediately show his critics in London that he was in control of his province. That meant he had to stay, for a time, at the center of government. During his first month in Pennsylvania, he, his family, and Logan lived in the house of Edward Shippen, the first mayor of Philadelphia. He then rented a large, comfortable house not far from the waterfront. There, on January 28, 1700, John Penn was born. He was to be the only one of Penn's children born in the New World.

"My wife is safely laid of a boy and both well for their time," Penn wrote to a friend in England. The relief he felt that Hannah delivered a healthy child was obvious in his words. Isaac Norris, a member of the Pennsylvania Assembly, described the new member of the Penn family as "a comely, lovely babe" and went on to say he hoped the child "will not want a good portion of his mother's sweetness, who is a woman extremely well beloved here, exemplary in her station, and of excellent spirit."[2]

Meanwhile, Penn threw himself wholeheartedly into the business of managing his province. By this time he was fifty-six years old. Though he probably never looked as stout as some artists have made him look, he was, no doubt, tending to chubbiness. Still, he had enough energy to work long hours and traveled great distances to get his colony's affairs in order.

As his first order of business, he summoned the legislative council to a meeting where he issued a proclamation condemning smuggling and piracy. He then convinced legislators to pass laws requiring all strangers and suspicious persons to explain who they were and what their business was to ferrymen and boatmen who brought them to the province and to innkeepers who provided them with lodging. At Penn's urging, a night watch was established to fight crime, which was beginning to be a problem in Philadelphia.

Such government interference in the business of the people went against Penn's beliefs. "I wish there were no need of any [government]," he told the provincial lawmakers, "but, since crimes prevail, government is made necessary by man's degeneracy."[3]

At the same time, Penn again tried to get the people of Pennsylvania to provide him with an income. "I have been now nineteen years your proprietor and governor, and have at my charge maintained my deputy, whereby I have much worsted myself and estate," he told them.[4] In response, the assembly approved a tax on imported liquors. This tax, they said, would net him about a thousand pounds a year in income. Unfortunately for Penn, they passed the tax, but took no steps to collect it.

Penn also had to deal with a request made by the council that a new Frame of Government be drawn up. He formed what he called a "grand committee" to study the charter and original Frame of Government "to keep what is good, in either, to lay aside what is inconvenient and burdensome, and to add to both what is best for the common good."[5] The committee could not come to any decision about how to change the Frame. Penn, in response, determined to rule the province according to the terms established by his original charter until such time as he drew up a new Frame of Government and submitted it to the legislators for their approval.

Penn's attempts to govern his province were complicated by the fact that the council and assembly were, at that time, divided into opposing political factions. Colonel Quary's Church of England Party was opposed by the Assembly Party, led by David Lloyd, the attorney general of the province. Both parties opposed much of what Penn wanted to do. For his part, Penn believed that political opposition was bad for the province because it led to dissension, which was anathema to a Quaker. In any case, according to his philosophy, since men of goodwill would always make the right decision if they were given free choice, dissension should be unnecessary. Now, faced with conflicts that wouldn't go away, he began to wonder if his beliefs were right. In an attempt to calm the dissension, he advised the members of the assembly and council "not to be easily displeased one with another," to be "slow to anger and swift to charity."[6]

These legislative battles were tiring, particularly in the heat of summer. Soon, the Penn family moved from the heat and clamor of the city to the cool and quiet of Pennsbury, making their way up the river in Penn's barge, outfitted with a mast and six oars. The barge was one of Penn's most prized belongings. He loved it, he said, "above all dead things."[7]

Hannah and Tish were, no doubt, favorably impressed as they landed at Pennsbury's small dock and made their way up the poplar-lined walkway to the manor's entrance. Entering the stately mansion they found, to the right, the best room and a dining hall, behind which were a pantry and kitchen. To the left was Penn's reception room, where he met government officials and Native American leaders who sometimes came to visit. Beyond that room were Penn's library and a private study. Upstairs were four large bedrooms and, on the third floor, more sleeping rooms and an attic.

Fortunately for Penn, the Quakers had no rules that Friends had to live simply and without pleasures, for throughout his life he always lived well. Except for his time in hiding, he managed to live in pleasant surroundings, if not luxury, and to enjoy the good things of life. Indeed, his financial woes were only made worse by his penchant for good living, since he often had to borrow to pay his living expenses. He continued living well in Pennsylvania, and Pennsbury soon was a center of hospitality in the province. The long dining table was often laden with platters of venison and turkey and vegetables grown in the garden behind the manor. For drink there was imported wine, home-brewed beer, cider made from Pennsbury apples, tea, coffee, and hot chocolate. The Penns, like virtually everybody in America in those days, usually ate from pewter plates, unless they had company, for whom Hannah would set the table with fine white and blue china. The family also had eight silver forks, a rarity in all but the wealthiest and most stylish colonial homes.

Penn made frequent trips from his comfortable estate to Philadelphia in the summer and fall of 1700, attending to the province's business. During this period, he completed negotiations with the chiefs of the Five Nations (the Iroquois) who granted him a deed for all the land in the Susquehanna Valley in central Pennsylvania.

It was at this time that Penn tried to improve the lot of slaves in the province. He proposed laws allowing them to marry. He thought the practice of splitting slave families apart was evil, and he asked that it be made illegal to divide slave families. He tried to pass laws so that slaves would be freed after a specified number of years and given some means of supporting themselves. With that in mind, he proposed that a six-thousand-acre township be set aside for former slaves, to be called Freetown. According to Quaker histories, Penn "mourned over the state of the slaves, but his attempts

to improve their condition by [law] were defeated."[8]
Indeed, these new attempts to help the slaves were voted
down by the assembly.

It should be noted that slaves owned by Quakers
were, for the most part, treated well. Friends believed
they owed their slaves not just decent physical treatment, but also spiritual care. Slaves accompanied their
masters to meeting on First Day and, eventually, had
their own meetings. Many Quakers freed their slaves
even though slaveholding was legal in the province until
the mid-1700s. A will written by Penn in 1701 indi-
cates that he himself freed the three or four slaves he
owned at the time.

In that same year, Penn learned from friends in England that his charter was again in jeopardy. For some
time, politicians in London had been in favor of ending all proprietorships in favor of royal provinces. Vir-
ginia, New York, and New Hampshire were already
royal colonies, Massachusetts had lost its proprietorship about ten years earlier, and Maryland, the colony
most like Pennsylvania in terms of its government, had
become a royal colony in 1692. Now Penn stood a good
chance of losing his province because of governmental
problems that just would not go away.

These troubles stemmed, in large part, from complaints that Colonel Quary had sent to Whitehall.
Among the complaints were charges that Pennsylvania
had an independent government that acted without
proper concern for English law. In addition, Quary said,
piracy went unchecked in the waters of the colony, and
Penn overstepped his bounds in making government
appointments.

Penn answered the charges as best he could, in writing. "We renounce all independency both as our duty

SIXTEEN

The Final Years

After a swift voyage, the *Dolmahoy* arrived in England on December 31, 1701. The ocean crossing had been untroubled by storms or pirates or illness other than the usual bouts of seasickness among the passengers. Just before the ship made landfall, however, Penn, less agile now that he was almost sixty years old, slipped on deck, injuring his leg so that he was limping as he walked down the gangplank in Portsmouth harbor.

Immediately, Penn, with Tish to care for him, rushed off to London where he once again took lodgings in Kensington, close to Court where he had so much business to transact. Hannah and two-year-old John went on to Bristol, to stay at the Callowhill home until Hannah gave birth.

In London, Penn found the English government ready to strip him of his province. Because of his injured leg, however, he was forced to spend several weeks resting before he could respond to charges that had been leveled against the provincial government by Colonel Quary. The situation grew even more serious when, on March 8, King William died, to be succeeded by his sister-in-law Anne.

The second daughter of James II, Anne was a strict Anglican. With her on the throne, there was a real chance that the oppression of religious dissenters that had been eased by William and Mary would resurface.

Penn quickly put his skills as a courtier to work, writing a greeting from "the people commonly called Quakers"[1] to the new queen. In that letter, he congratulated Anne, declared the loyalty of the Friends, and made a plea for continued toleration. The address to the queen worked its magic. "Mr. Penn," she said after the Quaker read it to her at Whitehall, " . . . you and your friends may be assured of my protection."[2]

On March 9, one day after the death of William III, while Penn was busy gaining Queen Anne's support, Hannah gave birth to a second son, Thomas. Penn, preoccupied with Quaker affairs, was unable to be by his wife's side when the child was born and, in fact, saw her only a few times during the first half of 1702. During those months, as he once again became a frequent visitor at Whitehall and gained favor at the Court, he was battered by personal misfortunes.

The first of these centered on the long-overdue debts he owed Philip Ford. Ford, Penn's longtime business agent, had died at about the time Penn returned to England. His widow, Bridget, now told Penn that documents he had signed for her husband gave her the right to sell Pennsylvania if he did not immediately pay his total debt to her. Penn quickly learned from attorneys he hired to protect his interests that Bridget Ford indeed had a case. The papers he had signed just before his second voyage to America were deeds giving Ford and his heirs ownership of the province.

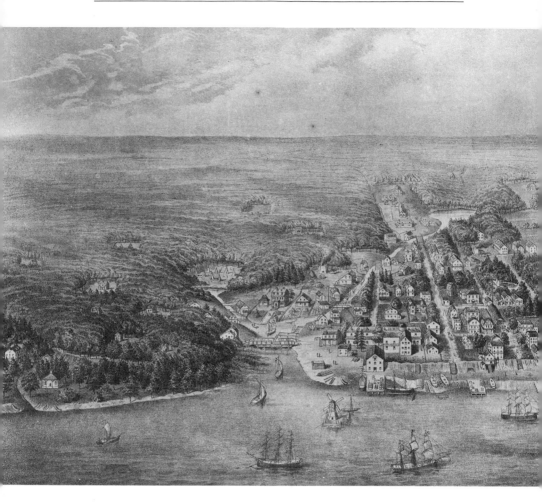

The sad reality was that, by 1702, Penn was almost without funds. For two decades he had received virtually no rents from Pennsylvania or from the lands he owned in Ireland and England. At the same time, as the Pennsylvania proprietor, he had paid all the expenses of his province for many years. In those years, he wrote about fifty books and pamphlets that he had printed at his own expense. He also financed many

A view of Philadelphia in 1702

other worthy Quaker causes. By the time Bridget Ford pressed her claim, he had no way of paying what she demanded, even if he had wanted to. He decided to fight her in court. It was a legal battle that would drag on for almost five years.

Then there was the matter of William Penn Jr., Penn's eldest son. To his father's dismay, Billy was decidedly un-Quakerish. A married man and, by this time, a father, he was a playboy who drank too much and persisted in piling up outrageous bills for his father to settle.

Somehow, Penn convinced himself that all Billy needed to grow up was a taste of responsibility in Pennsylvania. In early 1703, he ordered his son to go to the province and told him if he did not go, his debts would not be paid. Reluctantly, William Jr. agreed to the move. In late 1703, leaving his wife behind, probably to live with her parents, he sailed for the province in the company of John Evans, whom Penn had just named as deputy governor. The two men arrived in Philadelphia on February 2, 1704.

Even before Billy's departure, Penn, tired, discouraged, and nearly destitute, decided to give up his American province. On May 11, 1703 he told the Lords Commissioners of the Board of Trade and Plantations that he would sell his control of the government of Pennsylvania for "a reasonable satisfaction" provided he could retain "some few privileges that will not be thought, I believe, unreasonable."[3]

His asking price for Pennsylvania was thirty thousand pounds. The "few privileges" he wanted to retain were, basically, all the rights he enjoyed as proprietor. He must not have been surprised when the Crown refused his offer. Still, Penn had opened the door to an idea the politicians found attractive, and negotiations continued sporadically over many months.

At about this time, Penn traveled to Bristol to be with Hannah. He was with her in her father's house on July 30, 1703, when Hannah Margarita, the third child of Penn's second marriage, was born. Finally, a few months later, probably helped by his father-in-law, he was able to afford lodgings in London for himself, his wife, and children. Except for brief visits, it was the first time the family had been together since their landing almost two years earlier.

For a few months following that move, Penn seems to have enjoyed a period of peace. Negotiations with the Crown were moving ahead slowly, and, thanks to efforts by James Logan, he had sufficient money for his everyday needs. Then, in the fall of 1704, Penn received disturbing reports about Billy and Governor Evans.

Evans, it seems, had clashed with members of the Pennsylvania Assembly almost as soon as he stepped off the boat from England. One of his first official acts was to form a militia, a force of unpaid volunteers which he named the Governor's Guard. Virtually everybody in Pennsylvania was opposed to this move. The Quakers believed the militia violated the nonviolent beliefs on which the colony had been founded. Non Quakers were opposed because they viewed the militia as an armed force that Evans might use to impose his will on the population. Then, as if to add insult to injury, Billy Penn joined the militia and became its drillmaster.

But still worse was to come. In August 1704, Billy was involved in a tavern brawl. Had he not been Penn's son, he would have been charged with disorderly conduct. As it was, the scandalous news of the brawl spread like wildfire. "I wish things had been better, or he had never come," wrote one of the colony's leading Quakers shortly after the fracas.[4] "He is my greatest affliction, for his soul's and my country's and family's sake," Penn said.[5]

By late 1704, Penn had no choice but to order his son back to England. By that time, he was again living at Worminghurst with his family, larger now with the addition of a fourth child, Margaret. In January of the next year, Billy appeared at the manor house with a sword strapped to his waist. There, in the great hall that had been the scene of so many Quaker meetings, he told his father he was turning his back on the Quaker faith. He also announced his plans to run for Parliament, even though running for office meant he would be required to swear an oath, to take the very action his father and thousands of other Quakers had gone to prison to protest.

Penn, ever loyal, stood by his son even as Billy took steps that seemed designed to break his heart. It is to Penn's credit that he respected his son's decisions because he believed his son was acting in good faith. In any event, Billy lost his bid for election to Parliament. "I wish it [the loss of the election] might turn his face to privacy and good husbandry, if not to [the Friends]," his father said.[6]

Instead, William Penn Jr. decided—just as his father had done when he was a young man in Ireland—to become a career soldier. Penn once again supported his errant son as best he could, but he was heartbroken. "O Pennsylvania! what hast thou cost me?" he cried in a letter to James Logan. "Above thirty thousand pounds more than I ever got by it, two hazardous and most fatiguing voyages, my . . . slavery here, and my child's soul almost. . . ."[7]

During all these months, Bridget Ford had continued pressing her demands. After analyzing Ford's accounts, Penn and his lawyers had determined that Ford had charged too much interest on debts he was owed, neglected to credit payments made to him, and imposed outrageous fees for much of the work he did. Instead of fourteen thousand pounds, the amount Bridget Ford said she was owed, Penn's attorneys offered about forty-three hundred pounds. She refused to accept this offer and filed suit for the staggering sum of twenty thousand pounds. In 1706 the case was referred to the Chancery Court (civil court) which would ultimately hear it.

While Penn was dealing with provincial affairs and with his financial problems, he moved yet again, this time to lodgings in Ealing, about eight miles from London, while Hannah and the children returned again to her father's house in Bristol. There, in January 1706, she gave birth to another child, Richard. As soon as she was able, she and the children rejoined Penn.

For three more years, the Ford suit dragged on in court. Early in this period, Penn and his son sold the rights they shared in Worminghurst. This eased Penn's desperate need for money, at least for a time, but it did not solve his financial problems, which grew even more stringent with the birth, in 1707, of a seventh child, Dennis Penn. Some of his concerns about Pennsylvania, however, were eased at about the same time, when Evans finally overstepped his bounds as governor. Personally chasing a ship that had left Philadelphia without filing required papers, the governor had boarded it where it had taken refuge in a New Jersey port. Viewed as a blatant infringement of another colony's jurisdiction, this gave Penn an opportunity to discharge Evans from his post.

Finally, in November 1707, a ruling was handed down in Bridget Ford's lawsuit. Because the accounts were so tangled, the judges refused to examine them in detail. They ordered Penn to pay what she demanded or face imprisonment in the Fleet, the debtors' prison.

On January 7, 1708, Penn attended a meeting at Gracechurch Street, the place so central to so much of his Quaker history. In the midst of the meeting, bailiffs entered the building and tried to arrest him. His attorneys, who were with him, protested that a man of Penn's age and standing deserved better treatment. They convinced the bailiffs to leave, promising he would surrender before the day was out. A few hours later, William Penn became a prisoner once again.

He was not actually jailed but was placed on something like house arrest near the Fleet. He found what one visitor described as "commodious lodgings."[8] Still, he was not a free man, unable even to be with Hannah while their daughter, Hannah Margarita, then about four-and-one-half years old, was dying at Bristol, perhaps of smallpox.

Meanwhile, Friends and non-Friends throughout England came to Penn's aid as word spread of his arrest. Public opinion turned against Bridget Ford and her son, Philip Ford Jr. Even Queen Anne made her displeasure known when she angrily dismissed a petition written by the Fords asking her to grant them a new charter to Pennsylvania.

Suddenly, the Fords began to fear they might end up without either the province or any money from Penn. They quickly began negotiating a settlement, and, by the fall of 1708, they agreed to accept seventy-six hundred pounds as full payment of Penn's debts. Penn's friends immediately pooled enough money to pay the debt.

Hannah, meanwhile, had joined her husband in his lodgings near the prison. There, on September 5, shortly before the debt was paid and Penn released, a baby girl, named Hannah for her mother, was born. A sickly baby, this last child of William Penn's lived just a few weeks.

Not long after the baby's death, Hannah and the children moved back to her father's house, while Penn searched for a place to live in London. Letters written to Hannah at that time were filled with loving phrases and concern. His handwriting, though, was larger than it had been in the past, with uneven letters that showed he was losing some control of his hands. Still, he was able to return to his preaching, traveling throughout England when he wasn't searching for a home for his family.

In February 1710, he moved his entire family, including Billy and his wife and children, into a large home at Ruscombe, between London and Oxford. Once he and his family were settled in the countryside, Penn renewed his efforts to sell his proprietary rights in Pennsylvania to the Crown. A new governor, Charles Gookin, had been named by Penn. Unfortunately he, like his predecessors, was soon involved in disputes with the assembly. By this time, Penn was too tired for fighting and disputing. He was tired, too, of his inability to obtain revenues that he believed were his moral and legal right. Sixty-six years old, he wanted to rid himself of the exasperations and costs of the colonial experiment he now viewed as a failure.

In early 1711 it appeared that agreement with the Crown was near. Penn had lowered his price to twenty thousand pounds, to be paid over a period of seven years, and the Lords Commissioners had recommended to the queen that his terms be met. The queen's advisors, however, believed that Penn would accept a smaller amount. In June 1712, they offered to buy the province for twelve thousand pounds paid over four years. Penn soon accepted their offer, provided they paid him a thousand pounds immediately.

As soon as that advance was paid, while the final details of the purchase were still being discussed, Penn, Hannah, and the children made a visit to Bristol. There, on October 4, as Penn was writing a letter to James Logan, he suffered a severe stroke. He had already written four full pages and was starting a fifth when he lost consciousness. Hannah finished the letter, explaining Penn's stroke as a "lethargich illness" and expressing hope that he would get better. ". . . it has pleased the Lord . . . to shew us mercy; in the comfortable prospect of his recovery; though as yet but weak," she said.[9]

The stroke left Penn partially paralyzed and seemed also to have affected his mind. Although he recovered slightly, he was in no condition to transact business, and so the sale of his province was suspended, never to be completed.

The Penns remained at Bristol until late January 1713. At that time, Hannah took him back to London where he rallied briefly. The noise and excitement of the city proved to be more than he could cope with, though, and he returned to quiet, rural Ruscombe. "He just reached home, when he was seized by the same severe illness," Hannah later reported in a letter to Logan.[10]

This stroke left him incapacitated. For the balance of his life he depended on others for all his care. On occasion he would be taken in his carriage to a meeting at nearby Reading, but those who visited his bedside found that his mind wandered and he was unable to speak the powerful phrases that had convinced so many of the unconvinced and swayed the actions of the English Crown.

For the next six years, Penn's condition slowly worsened. Eventually, the great man became almost childlike. He often did not recognize Friends who came to his sickroom. Thomas Story, a good and loyal Friend from Philadelphia, came to visit and was stricken by what he saw. "When I went to the house I thought myself strong enough to see him in that condition," Story said, "but when I entered the room and perceived the great defect of his expressions, for want of memory, it greatly bowed my spirit. . . ."[11]

Finally, at about two-thirty on the morning of July 30, 1718, William Penn died peacefully. He was buried in the graveyard adjacent to Jordans Friends Meeting House. His grave, with a simple stone, was dug next to the grave of his first wife and near those of many of his children.

Soon after Penn's death, Quakers at the Meeting House in Reading, England, published this testimony.

> . . . He was learned without vanity, [easy] in conversation, yet weighty and serious . . . of an extraordinary greatness of mind, yet void of the strain of ambition; as free from rigid gravity as he was clear of unseemly levity; a man, a scholar, a friend, a minister surpassing in superlative endowments whose memorial will be valued by the wise. . . ."[12]

William Penn was all those things and more. To be sure, the holy experiment of Pennsylvania was never the utopia he hoped it would be. Still, in the process of founding a colony where men enjoyed more personal and religious freedom than had ever been known before, he blazed a path that was followed later by America's Founding Fathers. His courageous adherence to his beliefs no matter what the cost, his loving and just treatment of America's Indians, and his visionary ideas about world government provide lessons that still ring true even now, almost three hundred years after his death. For all these reasons, his life continues to stand as a shining example of courage and dignity and the possibilities of peace and loving tolerance.

Chronology

1642		English Civil War begins.
1644	*October 24*	William Penn is born in London.
1647/8		William has smallpox.
1649	*January 30*	King Charles I is executed in London.
1650	*(approx.)*	William begins education at Chigwell School.
1655		William's father is imprisoned.
1656	*August*	Penn family moves to Ireland.
1657		William hears the Quaker Thomas Loe speak at Macroom, Ireland.
1660	*March*	William returns to England. William's father is knighted by King Charles II.
	October 26	William enrolls in Oxford University.
1662	*March*	William is expelled from Oxford.
	July	William departs for France.
	Fall	William becomes a student at Saumur.
1664	*Winter*	William returns to England.

1665	*February*	William enrolls at Lincoln's Inn.
	June	The plague attacks London.
1666	*January*	William goes to Ireland.
	September	The Great Fire destroys much of London.
1667	*Summer*	William hears Thomas Loe speak again and becomes a convinced Quaker.
	September 3	William is arrested for the first time, imprisoned in Cork, Ireland.
	Fall	William returns to England.
1668	*Spring*	William meets Gulielma Springett.
	December 12	William is arrested in London.
1669	*Early Spring*	William writes *No Cross, No Crown* while a prisoner in the Tower of London.
	July 28	William is freed from the Tower.
1670	*Summer*	William is arrested for public preaching in London.
	September 5	William is sentenced to the Tower of London.
	September 16	Admiral Sir William Penn dies.
1671	*February*	William is arrested, imprisoned in Newgate.
	Summer	William is released from prison.
1672	*April 4*	William and Gulielma marry in Amersham, England.
1675	*February*	William writes New Jersey Charter.
1677	*July*	William travels as a missionary in Germany and Holland.
1680	*June 1*	William petitions King Charles for grant of land in America.
1681	*March 4*	William is granted Pennsylvania Charter.

1682	*March*	William's mother, Hannah Penn, dies.
	August 30	William departs from England for Pennsylvania.
	October 29	William lands on Pennsylvania soil.
	December 4	Pennsylvania's assembly meets for the first time.
1684	*August 12*	Penn leaves Pennsylvania for England.
1685	*February 6*	King Charles II dies, James II takes throne.
1687	*April*	King James suspends laws against religious nonconformists.
1688	*April*	King James is deposed in the Glorious Revolution. William is under investigation because of friendship with James.
1691	*January*	William goes into hiding to avoid trial.
1692	*Summer*	William is deprived of Pennsylvania.
	Summer-Fall	William writes *An Essay Towards the Present and Future Peace of Europe* and *Some Fruits of Solitude.*
1693	*Winter*	William is exonerated by King William.
1694	*February 23*	Gulielma, William's wife, dies.
	Summer	Pennsylvania is restored to William's ownership.
1696	*March 5*	William marries Hannah Callowhill.
	Winter	William proposes unified government for American colonies.
1699	*September 9*	William returns to Pennsylvania.
1701	*October 28*	Pennsylvania's Charter of Privileges is adopted.
	November	William returns to England with his family.
	Fall	William and Gulielma's son, William Jr., leaves England for Pennsylvania.

1704	*Winter*	William orders William Jr. home.
1705		Bridget Ford sues William for indebtedness.
	November	William is ordered to pay Bridget Ford.
1708	*January 7*	William is arrested, placed in debtor's prison.
	Fall	William's debt is settled.
1711	*October 4*	William suffers a stroke.
1713	*January*	William is stricken again and, this time, incapacitated.
1718	*July 30*	William Penn dies.

Source Notes

Chapter One

1. Quoted in Antonia Fraser, *Royal Charles: Charles II and the Restoration* (New York: Dell Publishing, 1979), p. 28.
2. Quoted in Fraser, p. 22.
3. Quoted in William Comfort, and others, *Remember William Penn* (Philadelphia: William Penn Tercentenary Committee, 1944), p. 2.
4. Quoted in Catherine Owens Peare, *William Penn: A Biography* (Ann Arbor: University of Michigan Press, 1966), p. 9.
5. Robert Latham, ed., *The Shorter Pepys* (Berkeley: University of California Press, 1985), p. 482.
6. Quoted in Harry Wildes, *William Penn* (New York: Macmillan Publishing Co., Inc., 1974), p. 9.
7. Quoted in Robert Gray, *A History of London* (London: Hutchinson & Co., 1978), p. 145.
8. Quoted in Comfort and others, p. 22 (Section B).
9. Quoted in Bonamy Dobree, *William Penn, Quaker and Pioneer* (Boston: Houghton Mifflin, 1932), p. 3.
10. Quoted in William Hull, *William Penn: A Topical Biography* (London: Oxford University Press, 1937), p. 68.
11. Oliver L. Dick, *Aubrey's Brief Lives* (London: Secker & Warburg, 1960), p. 234.
12. Quoted in Peare, p. 19.

13. Quoted in: Wildes, p. 16.
14. Quoted in Samuel M. Janney, *The Life of William Penn* (Freeport, NY: Books for Libraries Press, 1970), p. 14.

Chapter Two
 1. Quoted in Mabel Brailsford, *The Making of William Penn* (Freeport, NY: Books for Libraries Press, 1966), p. 60.
 2. Quoted in Brailsford, p. 62.
 3. Quoted in Samuel M. Janney, *The Life of William Penn* (Freeport, NY: Books for Libraries Press, 1970), p. 23.
 4. Quoted in Jessamyn West, ed., *The Quaker Reader* (Wallingford, PA: Pendle Hill Publications, 1992), p. 47.
 5. Quoted in Brailsford, p. 66.
 6. George Fox, *The Journal of George Fox* (New York: E.P. Dutton Everyman's Library, 1962), p. 34.
 7. Quoted in Brailsford, p. 77.
 8. Quoted in Bonamy Dobree, *William Penn: Quaker and Pioneer* (Boston: Houghton Mifflin Company, 1932), p. 8.
 9. Quoted in Dobree, p. 8.
10. Quoted in Dobree, p. 8.
11. Quoted in William Hull, *William Penn: A Topical Biography* (London: Oxford, 1937), p. 106.
12. Quoted in Antonia Fraser, *Royal Charles* (New York: Dell Publishing, 1979), p. 159.
13. Quoted in Catherine Owens Peare, *William Penn: A Biography* (Ann Arbor: University of Michigan, 1966), p. 26.

Chapter Three
 1. Quoted in William Comfort and others, *Remember William Penn* (Philadelphia: William Penn Tercentenary Committee, 1944), p. 11.
 2. Robert Latham, ed., *The Shorter Pepys* (Berkeley: University of California Press, 1985), p. 130.
 3. Samuel Janney, *Life of William Penn* (Freeport, NY: Books for Libraries Press, 1970), p. 23.
 4. Quoted in Bonamy Dobree, *William Penn: Quaker and Pioneer* (Boston: Houghton Mifflin Company, 1932), p. 11.
 5. Janney, p. 23.
 6. Quoted in Catherine Owens Peare, *William Penn: A Biography* (Ann Arbor: University of Michigan Press, 1966), p. 36.

7. Quoted in Peare, p. 37.
8. William Penn, *No Cross, No Crown* (Richmond, IN: Friends United Press, 1981), pp. 63–64.
9. Penn, p. 64.

Chapter Four
1. Robert Latham, ed., *The Shorter Pepys* (Berkeley: University of California Press, 1985), p. 419.
2. Latham, p. 418.
3. Quoted in Elizabeth Janet Gray, *Penn* (New York: Viking Press, 1962), pp. 56–57.
4. Quoted in Catherine Owens Peare, *William Penn: A Biography* (Ann Arbor: University of Michigan Press, 1966), p. 47.
5. Peare, p. 48.
6. Latham, p. 494.
7. Latham, p. 508.
8. Latham, pp. 515–516.
9. Samuel M. Janney, *The Life of William Penn* (Freeport, NY: Books for Libraries Press, 1970) p. 23.
10. Bonamy Dobree, *William Penn: Quaker and Pioneer* (Boston: Houghton Mifflin Company, 1932), p. 24.
11. Janney, p. 23.

Chapter Five
1. Robert Latham, ed., *The Shorter Pepys* (Berkeley: University of California Press, 1985), p. 662.
2. Quoted in Mabel Brailsford, *The Making of William Penn* (Freeport, NY: Books for Libraries Press, 1965), p. 168.
3. Quoted in Brailsford, p. 175.
4. Quoted in Brailsford, p. 175.
5. Catherine Owens Peare, *William Penn: A Biography* (Ann Arbor: University of Michigan Press, 1966), p. 57.
6. Quoted in Brailsford, p. 175.
7. Bonamy Dobree, *William Penn, Quaker and Pioneer* (Boston: Houghton Mifflin Company, 1932), p. 29.

Chapter Six
1. William W. Comfort and others, *Remember William Penn* (Philadelphia: William Penn Tercentenary Committee, 1944), p. 31.

2. Quote in Mabel Brailsford, *The Making of William Penn* (Freeport, NY: Books for Libraries Press, 1965), p. 176.

3. Quoted in Catherine Owens Peare, *William Penn: A Biography* (Ann Arbor: Univeristy of Michigan Press, 1966), p. 60.

4. Quoted in Peare, p. 60.

5. Quoted in Peare, p. 61.

6. Quoted in Hans Fantel, *William Penn: Apostle of Dissent* (New York: William Morrow & Co., 1974), p. 91.

7. Quoted in Peare, p. 65.

8. Quoted in Peare, p. 77.

9. Quoted in Peare, p. 83.

10. Quoted in Peare, p. 83.

11. Quoted in Peare, p. 84.

12. Quoted in Comfort and others, p. 32.

Chapter Seven

1. Quoted in *Samuel Janney, Life of William Penn* (Freeport, NY: Books for Libraries Press, 1970), p. 54.

2. Quoted in Catherine Owens Peare, *William Penn: A Biography* (Ann Arbor: University of Michigan Press, 1965), p. 104.

3. Quoted in Janney, pp. 57–58.

4. Quoted in William Comfort and others, *Remember William Penn* (Philadelphia: William Penn Tercentenary Committee, 1944), pp. 36–37.

5. Quoted in Comfort and others, p. 38.

6. Quoted in Comfort and others, p. 41.

7. Quoted in Comfort and others, p. 45.

8. Quoted in Janney, p. 73.

9. Quoted in Janney, p. 73.

10. Quoted in Peare, p. 125.

11. Quoted in Mabel Brailsford, *The Making of William Penn* (Freeport, NY: Books for Libraries Press, 1965), p. 329.

Chapter Eight

1. Quoted in William Hull, *William Penn: A Topical Biography* (London: Oxford University Press, 1937) pp. 66–67.

2. Quoted in Catherine Owens Peare, *William Penn: A Biography* (Ann Arbor: University of Michigan Press, 1966), p. 130.

3. Quoted in Samuel M. Janney, *The Life of William Penn* (Freeport, NY: Books for Libraries Press, 1970), p. 81.
4. Quoted in Janney, pp. 82–84.
5. Quoted in Hull, p. 194.
6. Quote in Hull, p. 195.
7. Quoted in Peare, p. 144.
8. Quoted in Hull, p. 33.

Chapter Nine
1. Quoted in Catherine Owens Peare, *William Penn: A Biography* (Ann Arbor: University of Michigan , 1966) p. 148.
2. George Fox, *The Journal of George Fox* (New York: E.P. Dutton & Company, 1963), pp. 316–317.
3. Fox, p. 319.
4. Quoted in Samuel M. Janney, *The Life of William Penn* (Freeport, NY: Books for Libraries Press, 1970), p. 102.
5. Quoted in Janney, p. 103.
6. Quoted in Janney, p. 103.
7. Quoted in Peare, p. 164.
8. Quoted in Peare, p. 197.
9. Quoted in Janney, p. 130.

Chapter 10
1. Quoted in William Hull, *William Penn: A Topical Biography* (London: Oxford University Press, 1937), p. 216.
2. Quoted in William Comfort and others, *Remember William Penn* (Philadelphia: William Penn Tercentenary Committee, 1944), p. 63.
3. Quoted in Catherine Owens Peare, *William Penn: A Biography* (Ann Arbor: University of Michigan Press, 1966), p. 209.
4. Quoted in Denis Meadows, *Five Remarkable Englishmen* (New York: Devin-Adair, 1961), p. 155.
5. Quoted in Comfort and others, p. 64.
6. Quoted in Comfort and others, p. 159.
7. Quoted in Comfort and others, p. 77.
8. Quoted in Peare, p. 229.
9. Quoted in Hull, p. 231.
10. Quoted in Hull, p. 336.

11. Quoted in Janney, p. 170.
12. Quoted in Peare, p. 225.
13. Quoted in Janney, p. 187.

Chapter Eleven
1. Quoted in William Comfort and others, *Remember William Penn* (Philadelphia: William Penn Tercentenary Committee, 1944), p. 84.
2. Quoted in Samuel Janney, *The Life of William Penn* (Freeport, NY: Books for Libraries Press, 1970), p. 196.
3. Quoted in Hans Fantel, *William Penn: Apostle of Dissent* (New York: William Morrow & Company, 1974), p. 192.
4. Quoted in Catherine Owens Peare, *William Penn: A Biography* (Ann Arbor: University of Michigan Press, 1966), p. 253.
5. Quoted in Peare, p. 264.
6. Quoted in Peare, p. 268.
7. Quoted in Harry Wildes, *William Penn* (New York: Macmillan Publishing Co., Inc., 1974), p. 194.
8. Quoted in William Hull, *William Penn: A Topical Biography* (London: Oxford University Press, 1937) p. 310.
9. Quoted in Fantel, p. 200.

Chapter Twelve
1. Quoted in Catherine Owens Peare, *William Penn: A Biography* (Ann Arbor: University of Michigan Press, 1966), p. 285.
2. Quoted in Samuel Janney, *The Life of William Penn*, (Freeport, NY: Books for Libraries Press, 1970), pp. 250–251.
3. Quoted in Janney, p. 253.
4. Quoted in Janney, p. 253.
5. Quoted in Janney, p. 258.
6. Quoted in Peare, p. 291.
7. Quoted in Janney, p. 260.
8. Quoted in Peare, p. 293.
9. Quoted in Janney, p. 271.
10. Quoted in Peare, p. 297.

Chapter Thirteen
1. Quoted in Samuel Janney, *The Life of William Penn* (Freeport, NY: Books for Libraries Press, 1970), p. 342.

2. Quoted in Janney, p. 349.
3. Quoted in Catherine Owens Peare, *William Penn: A Biography* (Ann Arbor: University of Michigan Press, 1966), p. 308.
4. Quoted in Janney, pp. 350–351.
5. Quoted in Janney, p. 353.
6. Quoted in Peare, p. 321.
7. Quoted in Peare, p. 323.
8. Quoted in William Comfort and others, *Remember William Penn* (Philadelphia: William Penn Tercentenary Committee, 1944), p. 124.
9. Quoted in Comfort and others, pp. 124–128.
10. Quoted in Comfort and others, p. 155.
11. Quoted in Comfort and others, Part II, pp. 7, 10, 13, 16, 41.
12. Quoted in Comfort and others, p. 155.
13. Quoted in Janney, p. 375.
14. Quoted in Janney, p. 378.

Chapter Fourteen
1. Quoted in Samuel Janney, *Life of William Penn* (Freeport, NY: Books for Libraries Press, 1970), p. 378.
2. Quoted in Catherine Owens Peare, *William Penn: A Biography* (Ann Arbor: University of Michigan Press, 1966), p. 334.
3. Quoted in Peare, p. 338.
4. Quoted in Peare, p. 343.
5. Quoted in Peare, p. 345.
6. Quoted in Peare, p. 350.
7. Quoted in William Comfort and others, *Remember William Penn* (Philadelphia: Penn Tercentenary Committee, 1944), pp. 143–144.
8. Quoted in Peare, p. 357.
9. Quoted in Peare, p. 364.
10. Quoted in Peare, p. 364.

Chapter Fifteen
1. Quoted in Samuel Janney, *Life of William Penn* (Freeport, NY: Books for Libraries Press, 1970), p. 404.
2. Quoted in Catherine Owens Peare, *William Penn: A Biography* (Ann Arbor: University of Michigan Press, 1966), pp. 369–370.

3. Quoted in Janney, p. 410.
4. Quoted in Janney, p. 411.
5. Quoted in Janney, p. 412.
6. Quoted in Janney, p. 413.
7. Quoted in Harry Emerson Wildes, *William Penn* (New York: Macmillan Publishing Co., 1974), p. 314.
8. Quoted in Janney, p. 423.
9. Quoted in Peare, p. 379.
10. Quoted in Janney, p. 431.
11. Quoted in Janney, p. 432.

Chapter Sixteen
1. Quoted in John Trussell, *William Penn: Architect of a Nation* (Harrisburg: Pennsylvania Historical and Museum Commission, 1974), p. 59.
2. Quoted in Samuel Janney, *Life of William Penn* (Freeport, NY: Books for Libraries Press, 1970), p. 443.
3. Quoted in Harry Wildes, *William Penn* (New York: Macmillan Publishing Co., Inc., 1974), p. 351.
4. Quoted in Janney, p. 467.
5. Quoted in Janney, p. 468.
6. Quoted in Wildes, p. 361.
7. Quoted in Catherine Owens Peare, *William Penn: A Biography* (Ann Arbor: University of Michigan Press, 1966) p. 394.
8. Quoted in Peare, p. 402.
9. Quoted in Peare, p. 412.
10. Quoted in Peare, p. 413.
11. Quoted in Peare, p. 414.
12. Quoted in William Comfort and others, *Remember William Penn* (Philadelphia: William Penn Tercentenary Committee, 1944), p. 11.

Bibliography

WILLIAM PENN BIOGRAPHIES

Brailsford, Mabel. *The Making of William Penn*. Freeport NY: Books for Libraries Press, 1966.

Dobree, Bonamy. *William Penn, Quaker and Pioneer*. Boston: Houghton Mifflin Company, 1932.

Fantel, Hans. *William Penn: Apostle of Dissent*. New York William Morrow & Co., 1974.

Hull, W. *William Penn: A Topical Biography*. London: Oxford University Press, 1937.

Janney, S.M. *The Life of William Penn*. Freeport, NY: Books for Libraries Press, 1970).

Meadows, D. *Five Remarkable Englishmen*. 1961.

Peare, Catherine Owens. *William Penn: A Biography*, Ann Arbor: University of Michigan Press, 1966.

Trussell, J. *William Penn: Architect of a Nation*. Harrisburg: Pennsylvania Historical and Museum Commission, 1974.

WILLIAM PENN'S WRITINGS
(SECONDARY SOURCES)

Comfort William, and others. *Remember William Penn*. Philadelphia: William Penn Tercenenary Committee, 1944.

> This is a marvelous collection of selections from Penn's writings along with commentary.

Selleck, R., ed., (William Penn) *No Cross, No Crown*. 1981.

West, J., ed., *The Quaker Reader*. 1992.

OTHER SECONDARY SOURCES

Boorstin, D.J., *The Americans: The Colonial Experience*. 1958.

Bray, W., Ed., *The Diary of John Evelyn*. 1895.

Carkeet-James, E.H., *Her Majesty's Tower of London*. 1953.

Carlton, C., *Charles I, the Personal Monarch*. 1995.

de Hartog, J., *The Peaceable Kingdom*. 1971.

Dunn, R.S. and M.M., *The World of William Penn*. 1986.

Fox, George. *The Journal of George Fox*. New York: E.P. Dutton & Co., 1962.

Fraser, Antonia. *Cromwell, the Lord Protector*. 1973.

———. *Faith and Treason: The Story of the Gunpowder Plot*. 1996.

———. *King James VI of Scotland–I of England*. 1975.

———. *Royal Charles: Charles II and the Restoration*. New York: Dell Publishing, 1979.

Gray, R. *A History of London*. 1978.

Hibbert, Christopher. *Tower of London*. 1971.

Hill, C. *The Century of Revolution, 1603–1714*. 1980.

Hutton, R. *Charles the Second*. 1989.

Latham, Robert, ed. *The Shorter Pepys.* Berkeley: University of California Press, 1985.

Meinig, D.W. *The Shaping of America, Vol. 1.* 1986.

Miers, E.S., ed. *The American Story.* 1956.

Moody, T.W. and Martin, F.X., *The Course of Irish History.* 1984.

Morgan, T. *Wilderness at Dawn.* 1993.

Morison, S.E. *The Oxford History of the American People.* 1965.

Morrill, J. *The Oxford Illustrated History of Tudor & Stuart Britain.* 1996.

Porter, R. *London: A Social History.* 1995.

Quinn, A. *A New World,* 1995.

Street, L. *An Uncommon Sailor: A Portrait of Admiral Sir William Penn,* 1988.

Wright, L.B. *Life in Colonial America,* 1971.

Index